W9-BFW-653

VENETIAN GLASS

VENETIAN GLASS

Confections in Glass

1855–1914

by Sheldon Barr

Preface by Marjorie Reed Gordon

Principal photography by John Bigelow Taylor

Photograph Credits

Principal photography is by John Bigelow Taylor. In addition to credit information provided in the captions, the following credits are herewith noted. Page 17: From J. B. Waring: *Masterpieces of Industrial Art and Sculpture at the International Exhibition,* 1862, vol. II, London, 1893, plate 280. Page 22: Courtesy Kenneth J. Lesko. Page 26: From *The Art Journal Catalogue of the Universal Exhibition,* London, 1868, p. 33. Pages 33, 34: Courtesy Alessandro Zoppi, Antichita Cesana, Venice. Pages 38, 60, 69, 80, 98, 99: Photograph Noel Allum

Page 1: Artisti Barovier. MOSAIC GLASS VASE. 1914. H. 6". Mark: murrhine bearing initials "AMF" and date "1914". Collection Usha Subramaniam, New York

Pages 2–3: Fratelli Toso. Mosaic glass details. 1900–1914. Collection Gardner & Barr, New York

Library of Congress Cataloging-in-Publication Data

Barr, Sheldon, 1938–
Venetian glass : confections of the glassmaker's art / by Sheldon Barr ; preface by Marjorie Reed Gordon ; principal photography by John Bigelow Taylor.
p. cm.
Includes bibliographical references.
ISBN 0-8109-3939-8 (clothbound)
1. Glassware—Italy—Venice. I. Title.
NK5152.V46B39 1998
748.295'31—dc21 97-32238

Published in 1998 by Harry N. Abrams, Incorporated, New York

Printed and bound in Hong Kong

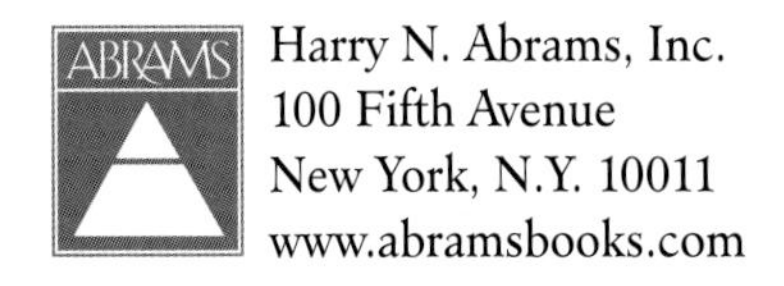

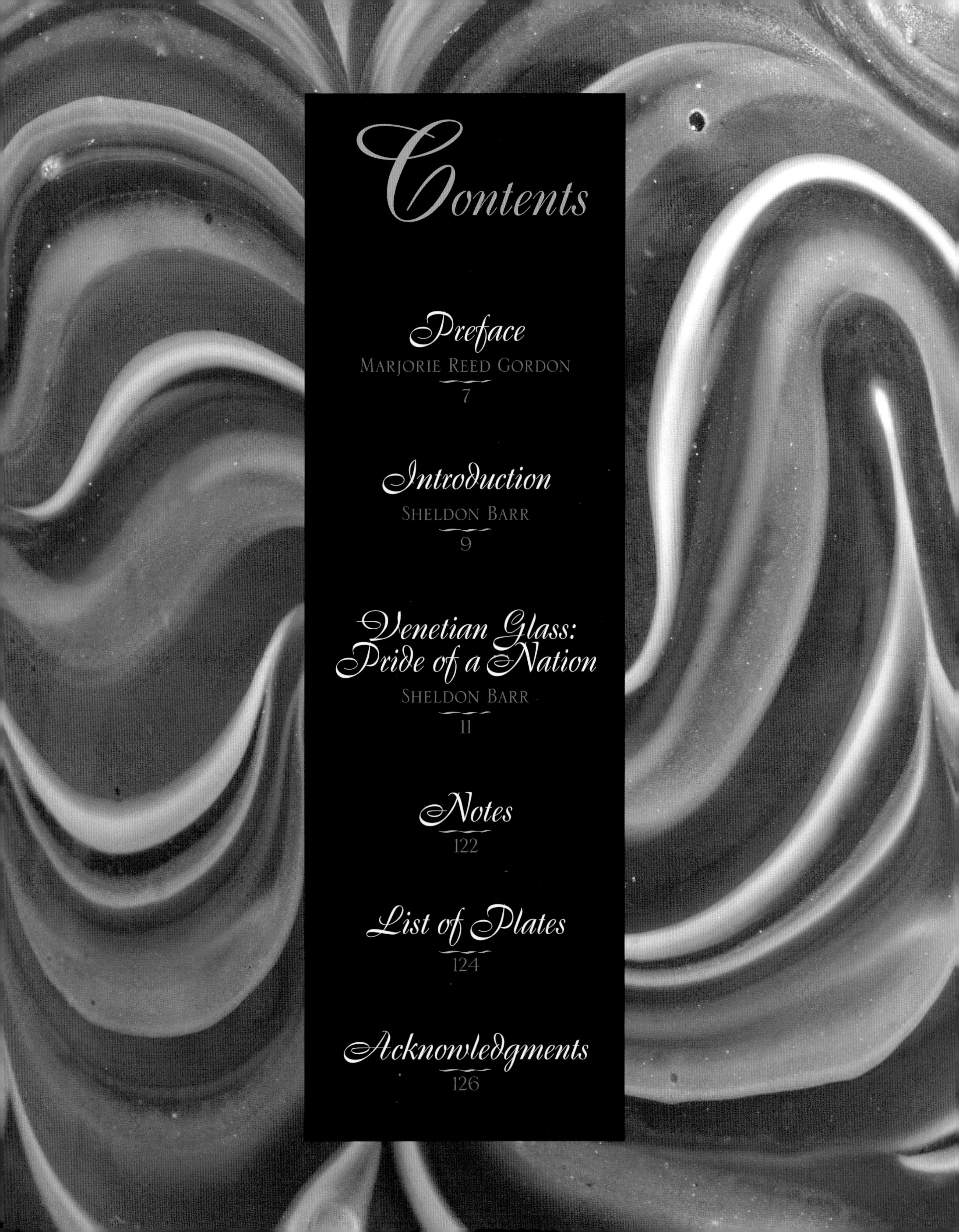

Contents

BY MARJORIE REED GORDON

AH VENICE! A BIT OF BYZANTIUM NESTLED IN AN ADRIATIC LAGOON. VENICE HAS HAUNTED MY dreams since I first visited there more than four decades ago. The peculiar alchemy of Italian sun mixing with mist rising from the canals creates an illumination that has enchanted visitors for centuries. Artist and artisan alike have been so inspired by this eerie light that they have made capturing it their life's work.

From its inception, Venice has enjoyed the enviable position of resting at the crossroads of East and West. It is no accident, then, that the culture which subsequently evolved owes much to both Europe and Asia. The art of glassmaking is a fine example of this as its roots can be traced to the earliest glass blowing techniques, a legacy of the ancient Romans and the design elements adapted from the Islamic glass of Asia Minor.

My earliest memories of Venetian glass can be traced to a pair of brilliant yellow, flowered compotes purchased by my grandmother at Salviati. As a little girl standing on tiptoe to watch the sunlight dance through these pieces, I was transfixed by their beauty. I thought that the sun itself had been somehow trapped inside of them. Years later, when my mother gave them to me, these compotes became the foundation upon which I built my collection.

Perhaps the greatest satisfaction I derive from collecting this glass lies in my treating each piece as an artifact that calls to mind a special Venetian moment. Staring at one piece I am carried to a secluded piazza dappled in sunlight and shadow. In another, I visualize the bobbing gondolas on the Grand Canal as the waves lap merrily at their hulls. In my mind's eye each goblet is filled with the ice cold bellini that awaits me on the terrace of the Gritti Hotel after a long day's meandering. The fanciful stone creatures which adorn my favorite palazzi are captured in the sinuous stems of my glasses and candlesticks. When I set my table with Venetian glass, I fantasize that I am a guest in the Doge's palazzo attending an eighteenth-century banquet. The table is richly draped in silk velvet, and each place is laid with seven glasses for the wines which will accompany each course. The vast hall is alive with the flickering light of hundreds of candles in delicate chandeliers. The telephone rings, and, with it, my reverie dissolves.

Apart from these flights of fancy, I find the search for additions to my collection enormously fulfilling. My passion for finding new pieces has carried me from five A.M. hunts by flashlight in country antique fairs to dusty Parisian curio shops. Although I have had good success all over the world, most of my collection is from various parts of America. There is ample reason for this. Like my grandmother, many Americans made the Grand Tour of Europe. A very popular souvenir was Venetian glass—so much so that nearly eighty percent of all the glass produced during this era wound up in the United States. One color, in fact, was called Rosso Americano based on its popularity with American buyers.

For many years, Venetian glass was out of fashion here, and subsequent generations stored the glass away in dusty attics, garages, and pantry closets. There it lies, waiting to be discovered. Here's hoping you don't get to it before I do!

Artisti Barovier or Fratelli Toso. COMPOTE WITH FLOWERS. 1895–1914. H. 8¼", Diam. 7½".
Collection Marjorie Reed Gordon, New York

Introduction

My greatest thrill has always been the thrill of discovery. I like nothing more than unearthing forgotten treasures. Perhaps I should have been an archaeologist, but dusty digging in hot climates just didn't appeal to me. I opted to pursue my explorations in big, modern cities. My first love was Tiffany glass. A pioneer in that intriguing treasure hunt, I remained enthralled with Mr. Tiffany's iridescent, mysterious creations for decades. When, about ten years ago, I realized that there was no more Tiffany glass to discover, or at least not enough to hold my interest, I began to cast about for something else to hunt for. I tried this and I tried that, but nothing equaled the thrill of discovering the muted lustre of Tiffany's glass still glowing under a half century's accumulation of grime. One day, not too long ago, I spotted an intriguing piece of glass at an obscure flea market in France. It was totally unlike the simply shaped, brilliantly colored iridescent glass that Tiffany produced. This bizarre object was the most complex glass creation I had ever seen. It was laden with glass dragons and serpents and I loved it. Your home-grown Howard Carter had found his personal Tutankhamen—Antonio Salviati. Well, I bought it, completely ignorant of just exactly who made it and how old it was. So began the quest for knowledge that eventually led me to write this book.

It became obvious to me from the onset that this extremely creative movement has been unjustly neglected and trivialized. Young collectors have an uncanny ability to look at old things with new eyes. Objects that seemed ugly to their parent's generation are suddenly infused with new glamor. When I began to stock my shop with Venetian glass, mixed in with Tiffany's creations, it was the Tiffany glass that began to look fussy and stale.

By the mid-19th century, Venice's ancient craft of glassmaking was dangerously close to extinction. A few adventurous souls, most notably Antonio Salviati, mounted a huge effort and succeeded in reviving the glass industry. His glass craftsmen and his competitors produced a large volume of late 19th- and early 20th-century glass that won critical and public acclaim, eventually finding its way into major museums and private collections throughout the world. Years passed and fashions changed and post World War II tastemakers passed their subjective judgment on art objects they perceived of as superfluous. Venice's superb glass was banished from view along with many another misunderstood treasure.

So they come down to us, this cavalcade of goblets, vases, decanters and chandeliers, dripping with dolphins and dragons, swans and serpents and storks, incredibly embellished with filigree and aventurine, perfect reminders of a more innocent time when romance and fantasy held sway.

Sheldon Barr
New York City

Artisti Barovier. Benvenuto Barovier, maker. Vetro a retorti Aventurine Vase with Dolphin Stem. 1895–1914. H. 10⅝". Collection Gardner & Barr, New York

An almost identical vase by Benvenuto Barovier but with a winged dragon and serpent stem is in a Barovier family collection.

Venetian Glass: Pride of a Nation

VENETIAN GLASS HAS BEEN FAVORED BY ROYALTY AND COMMONERS AS WELL for more than six hundred years. Its glorious colors, dazzling designs and patterns, and technical acrobatics in glass result in objects that delight and amaze us. Seemingly spun out of sugar, it's no wonder that Venetian glass is often thought of as confections of the glassmaker's art. For art it is: each object is unique and bears the remarkable stamp of the glass artisan who created it. Adornments such as dragons, serpents, birds, and flowers make up the stems, rims, and forms of so many objects, from the most breathtakingly delicate to the near-gaudy and outrageous. A heroic last-minute effort saved this endangered art from extinction in the mid-1800s. Much of the Venetian glass created then owes its forms and techniques to glass created centuries earlier by the Phoenicians, Romans, and Renaissance Venetians. But as always happens when artistic talents are allowed to flourish, the greatest of Venice's glassmakers began to produce objects distinctly of their own time and style. Not only was a renaissance in glassmaking born but an industry was created whose stature and output continues to this day.

The history of this remarkable glass begins one thousand years ago, when all of Europe except for Venice was still mired in the Dark Ages. Around that time, the tiny, secluded Venetian Republic had built her power base, an enormous, almost invincible fleet of ships. Brilliantly, and with more than a little duplicity, Venice maneuvered herself into position as the world's leading military and mercantile power. Venice's sovereignty began in 697 and endured an astounding eleven hundred years. Isolated in her lagoon and insulated from attack, rarely challenged and never conquered, Venice maintained easy possession of her riches. By the end of the fourteenth century, Venice had defeated her seafaring competitors, established a mainland empire, and was the hub of all contact, commercial and cultural, between Europe and the affluent kingdoms of the East. Local industries developed and, thanks to Venice's well established and secure trade routes, prospered. On the nearby

Left to right: The Venice and Murano Glass Company Limited (Salviati & C.). CRESTED EWER. 1872–77. H. 11". Salviati Dott. Antonio. DOLPHIN PITCHER WITH SERPENT HANDLE. 1883–95. H. 10". Artisti Barovier or Fratelli Toso. DRAGON-HANDLED EWER. 1895–1914. H. 12½". Collection Gardner & Barr, New York
The crested ewer is a faithful reproduction, except for its remarkable color, of a seventeenth-century original in the Murano Glass Museum. The dolphin pitcher is offered for sale in both the Salviati Dott. Antonio glassworks catalogue and the post-1883 Testolini shop's retail catalogue and confirms the fact that the Baroviers sold their production to other retail glass establishments after taking over the Salviati glassworks in 1883.

Venetian island of Murano, a startling glass production grew and eventually this glass became one of the Renaissance world's most coveted treasures.

No industry could have been better suited to this island nation of limited landmass. Sand and other raw materials for glassmaking were plentiful and, for a time, the limited space required for glass manufacture was available. A romantic late nineteenth-century notion held that the Venetian glassblowers were descended from Romans who had inhabited the town of Aquileia, a glassmaking center on the northeastern shore of the Adriatic. Fleeing the surging hordes of Barbarians marching south to pillage a weak and vulnerable fifth-century Rome, the glassmakers were reputed to have been driven, along with the citizens of other mainland Roman cities and towns, to find refuge on the isolated and underpopulated islands in the Venetian lagoon. The citizens of Aquileia would have brought to the islands centuries of glassmaking knowledge—especially the technique of glassblowing, invented about 50 B.C. in Phoenicia and perfected by the Romans in the first century A.D. Romanticized Roman origins aside, there is evidence of glass manufacture in Venice dating from the ninth century.

After the sack of Byzantium in 1204, Constantinople's glassmakers migrated to Venice bringing new techniques and fresh ideas. By the end of the thirteenth century, Venice had become the most important and crowded glassmaking center in Europe. Glassmakers were leaving the city and settling on Murano in large numbers. In 1291 this voluntary emigration became compulsory. Venice's *Maggior Consiglio,* or Grand Council, commanded the remaining glassmakers to extinguish their fires and join their comrades on the island. Murano became the glassmakers "gilded cage"; once there, they were forbidden by law to leave. Historians have pondered the reasons behind the council's decree for centuries. Some have argued that the danger of fire from the glassmakers' wood-burning furnaces presented too high a risk to Venice and her increasing concentration of magnificent buildings. More likely, the council, seeking to safeguard Venice's extremely lucrative glassmaking monopoly, decided to imprison the glassmakers along with their secrets on the easily secured island.

In an attempt to soften the glassmakers' confinement, the council granted privileges unique in the restricted class society of the period. The sons of Venetian nobles could marry the daughters of glassmakers without endangering their titles or the nobility of their children. In addition, the glassmakers were permitted to participate in the splendid Venetian pageants where they would proudly display masterpieces of their work—mirrors, blown glassware, mosaics, and fine beads.

Nevertheless, many glassmakers hated confinement and dared escape. As a result of their cunning departures, Venetian glassmaking techniques by the mid-fourteenth century had spread throughout Europe. In the eighteenth century, with Venice's economy in shambles and glassmaking its only viable industry, the draconian Grand Council sent assassins to hunt down and kill escapees if the prior measure of imprisoning close relatives failed to motivate their return.

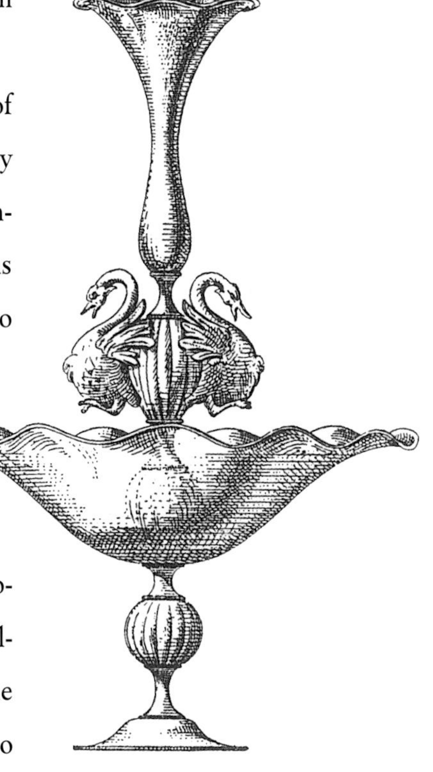

Royal Patrons

In the sixteenth and seventeenth centuries, the sequestered glassblowers of Murano produced an astounding variety of glass fantasies that adorned the palaces of Europe's nobility as well as the opulent homes of the rich bourgeoisie. The refined tastes of the Renaissance demanded a high level of artistic and technical perfection from the Murano masters, which they satisfied with astonishing virtuosity. Many forms that are still in use today—scallop shell vases, footed goblets and bowls, pilgrim flasks, hexagonal goblets, ewers and tazzas—were invented or elaborated from ancient models. A dazzling array of new techniques, enameled and engraved glassware, chalcedony, filigree, aventurine and ice glass, were invented and perfected. Murano's glass became so irresistible that by 1542 goblets had reached as far north as the court of Henry VIII in England and as far east as the palaces of Suleiman I, the Magnificent, in Constantinople. Poisonings were a common occurrence in sixteenth-century royal courts, and an elaborate lore surrounded Murano's glassware. These magical goblets, it was said, would spontaneously shatter if a mere drop of poisoned wine was poured into one. It's understandable why every paranoid potentate wanted some. If they didn't work, well, who would complain?

King Henri III of France arrived in Venice for his first state visit in 1574. Planning had gone on for months and the old republic, summoning up all the oriental pomp and splendor she was famous for, staged a spectacle so memorable that Venetians still talk of it today. Understandably, Venice was immensely proud of her glassmaking skills and never wasted an opportunity to show them off. The young king, escorted by hundreds of splen-

did craft, gilded and adorned with carved sea monsters, dolphins, and gods, was treated to a remarkable sight. The doge, Alvise Mocenigo, had provided a bizarre barge, carrying a functioning glassblower's furnace in the form of a large fire-breathing sea monster, flames belching from its mouth and nostrils. There, toiling in the heat, the glassblowers of Murano, with great bravura, were creating glass fantasies for the amusement of the delighted king and his entourage. It's no wonder that the entire Renaissance world stood in awe of this extraordinary glass.

More than a source of civic pride, Murano's glass industry was decidedly profitable. Exploring new trade possibilities, Venice's huge fleet of ships exchanged glassware for valuable spices and sumptuous fabrics for centuries. Venice's maritime dominance however, could not last forever. In the late fifteenth century, Portuguese navigator Vasco da Gama opened a sea route to India around the Cape of Good Hope. Venice's trade monopoly with the East had finally been broken and a slow, inexorable three hundred-year decline set in. Venice, *La Serenissima Repubblica* (serene because of her invulnerability in her protective lagoon), now faced increasing competition from other nations and threats to her power.

By the eighteenth century, Venice's industries—spice trade, wool production, and shipbuilding—had irrevocably declined and she had lost most of her colonial empire to the Turks. Glass, however, was such a desired trading commodity that its manufacture persisted even as Venice's fortunes faded. Having never been conquered nor plundered, La Serenissima was bloated with the wealth of centuries. In a decadent, hedonistic frenzy Venice began to squander her riches. Huge, luxurious new palaces were built and and existing ones enlarged, rebuilt and redecorated. Giant floating chandeliers, seemingly crafted of multicolored spun sugar, shimmering with candles and glass flowers, were commissioned from the Murano furnaces to ornament these sumptuous palazzi. Festivals became more and more glittering and frequent. Carnival lasted for six months and legend has it that the last one was the most opulent ever. Venice danced at her masked balls while the storm clouds gathered unnoticed (or rather, unheeded) around her. In May 1797, Napoleon Bonaparte, on his campaign to conquer Europe, anchored the French fleet off Venice. At first the terrified populace resisted Napoleon's advances, but then, almost nonchalantly, they surrendered. The Venetian republic as it was known had collapsed; this factor, plus the subsequent dominations by France and Austria virtually wiped out the glass industry by the mid-nineteenth century.

The Wreak of Austrian Occupation

Although some glass manufacturing continued through the confusing years of the early nineteenth century, the Austrian occupation was a period of regression for Venice's glass industry. By midcentury the number of operating glass furnaces had been significantly reduced and the production of luxury glass had stopped altogether. The worst was yet to come. After a failed attempt to free herself from Austria in 1848, Venice again succumbed. Vengeful Austria was determined to ruin the Venetian glass industry in favor of her own Bohemian glass factories. In order to accomplish this end Austria enacted destructive tariffs on both the import of raw materials and the export of finished glassware. Venice, by this time virtually devoid of natural resources, was forced to import sand from the Fontainebleau quarries in France and wood from Dalmatia and Istria.[1] The Austrians taxed them all heavily and made continued glass production profitless. Ultimately, the proud Murano glass industry, once furnisher of fabulous glassware to emperors, popes, and kings, was reduced to producing glass beads for Austria's colonial trade and poor quality utilitarian glassware, occasionally and understandably enameled with anti-Austrian sentiment. Fortunately, the political ferment of the mid-nineteenth century was soon to change everything.

Salviati and Radi Resurrect the Glass Industry

Arguably the pivotal event in the rebirth of the Venetian glass industry took place in 1859 when Dr. Antonio Salviati, a Venetian lawyer, founded a company called Salviati Dott. Antonio fu Bartolomeo.[2] Appalled by the devastation that decades of neglect had caused to the antique mosaic decoration of Venice and of St. Mark's Basilica in particular, Salviati sensed a unique opportunity. Encouraged by Antonio Colleoni, the mayor of Murano, and a local priest, Abbot Vincenzo Zanetti, he gave up the legal profession and began what was to be a celebrated career in glass with this new enterprise. The initial thrust of the company was the commercial production of glass mosaics for churches and public buildings and the manufacture of glass tesserae (bits of opaque colored glass used in the creation and restoration of mosaics). Both the showroom (Stabilimento Salviati)[3] and the factory were in Venice at Dorsoduro 731. Salviati engaged Roman mosaicist Enrico Podio as art director and as his collaborator the visionary glass technician Lorenzo Radi, who had been researching new colors for glass tesserae for twenty years. Embroiled in the fashionable nineteenth-century preoccupation of "historismus,"[4] Radi was a dedicated researcher of forgotten glassmaking techniques. In 1856, after years of research and experimentation, he succeeded in rediscovering the relatively simple process necessary to create examples of antique Venetian blown *calcedonio* (chalcedony) glass. Essentially, Radi was copying copies. The Venetian glassmasters of the late fifteenth through the early eighteenth century, inspired by ancient Roman and Byzantine banded agate vessels preserved in the treasury of St. Mark's Basilica, had mastered the art of creating glass that resembled stone. Ordinarily, in preparing the "melt" used to produce conventional glass, sand is fused to produce a pot-metal of homogeneous color, which is not suitable for creating chalcedony glass. Radi, however, by carefully melting shards of glass of different colors together and ensuring that the colors did not blend before blowing, created chalcedony glass for the first time in over one hundred years.

Having initially been brought together by their mutual interest in mosaic production, Radi and Salviati set up a small furnace for the production of chalcedony and other imitation stone blown glass in the mosaic factory adjoining their new shop.

Success came quickly. In 1861, the firm's gold, silver, and polychrome mosaic tesserae were considered fine enough to be used in the restoration of St. Mark's Basilica. A year later, already employing over two hundred mostly mosaic workers, Salviati and Radi earned their first gold medal at London's International Exhibition of 1862 where they presented their mosaic and glass production to the world. The South Kensington Museum, now the Victoria & Albert Museum, bought a superb metal-mounted chalcedony vase from Salviati at the exhibition. One of the highlights of the Salviati exhibit was a remarkable mosaic-topped table with a carved wood base incorporating five of Radi's chalcedony glass vases. Shortly after, Abbot Zanetti organized the *Prima Exposizione Vetreria* (First Glass Exhibition) in Murano in November 1864. The Salviati company exhibited and won first place for its mosaics and "vases of various shapes and sizes imitating chalcedony."[5]

The production of chalcedony glass was taken up by others, notably after 1866 by the Barovier family of glassblowers at Salviati's new company and later, from 1880, by the firm of Francesco Ferro e Figlio. Exciting new chromatic combinations, often incorporating bits

Salviati Dott. Antonio fu Bartolomeo. Lorenzo Radi, Domenico, and Antonio Giobbe, makers. MOSAIC TABLE TOP AND STAND. Diam. 41¾". 1859–62.
The highlight of Salviati's presentation at London's 1862 exhibition was this table, whose Moorish-inspired geometric mosaic top, which includes bits of Lorenzo Radi's chalcedony glass, reflects the advanced state Salviati and Radi had achieved in mosaic art. The base incorporates five of Radi's chalcedony glass vases. With this Salviati was able to, in his words, "manifest the good taste particular to Italy."

of aventurine glass, *filigrana* (filigree), or murrhine were developed. Severely limited by the character of the melt, chalcedony was always produced in very simple, classic shapes. Rare today, most surviving examples are preserved in museums and private collections.

Seeking to increase public awareness of his work in Britain, Salviati donated examples of the firm's blown glass production to The South Kensington Museum. In 1864 the firm presented Queen Victoria with a mosaic portrait of Prince Albert, her recently deceased husband. Soon, with both public and royal recognition assured, the Salviati firm was busy installing elaborate mosaic decoration on the vaulted ceiling and west wall of the Albert Chapel at Windsor Castle, the cupola of Saint Paul's Cathedral, and the atrium of the Houses of Parliament in London as well as embellishing the Albert Memorial and The South Kensington Museum. Salviati and his production became celebrated in Britain and he soon opened his first London showroom at 431 Oxford Street. In Paris, Salviati engaged the renowned glass shop L'Escalier de Crystal[6] to sell the firm's production of mosaics and blown glass.

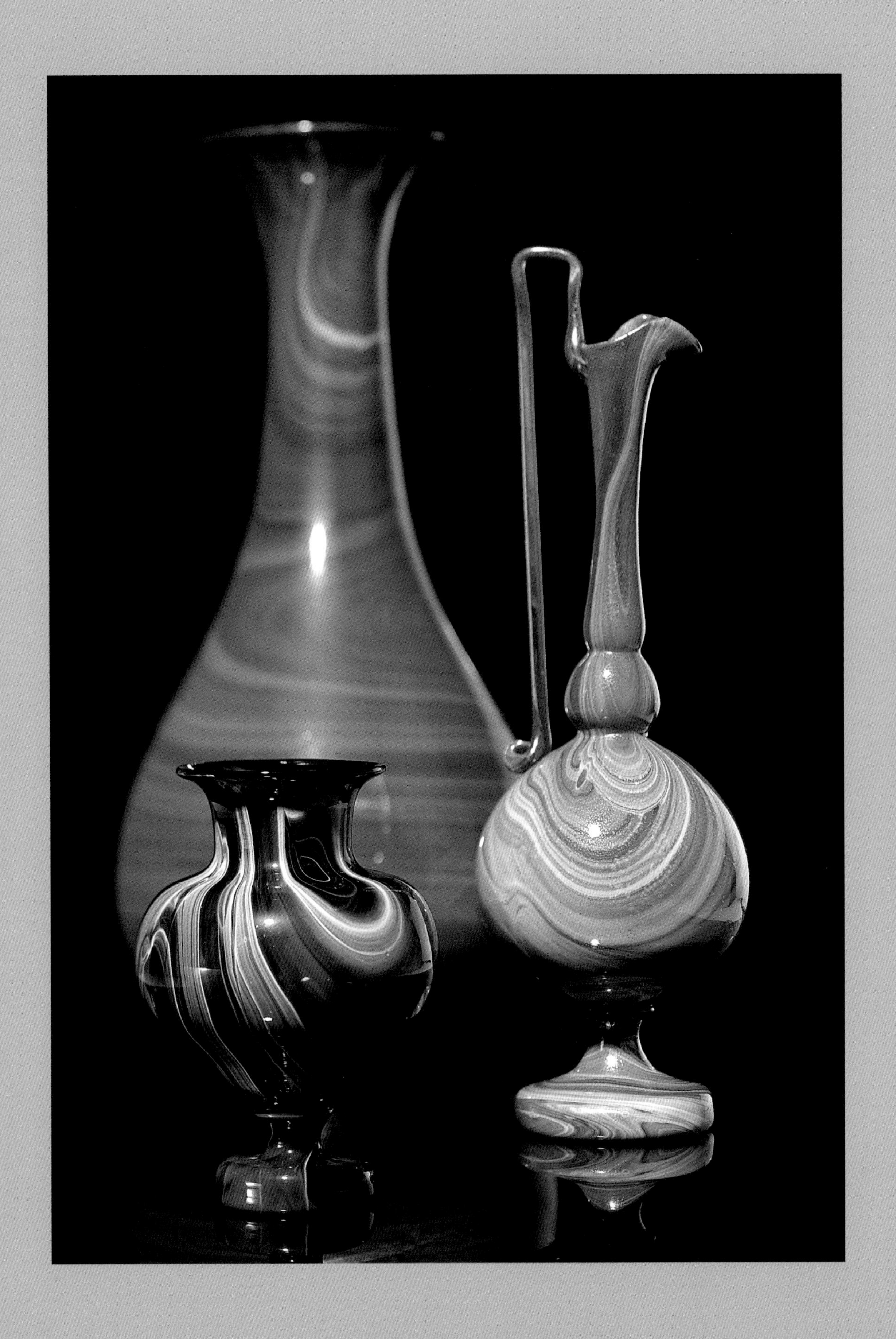

A Last-Minute Rescue

In the early 1860s, with the realization that the great, centuries-old glassmaking heritage of Murano was about to be lost, Mayor Colleoni, Abbot Zanetti, and Salviati mobilized into action. Colleoni and Zanetti began the preservation effort by collecting documents relating to the history of glassmaking on the island and searching out and purchasing the best examples of antique Murano glass they could find. By 1861 the two had inaugurated a glass museum on Murano, initially for the instruction of young glassmakers and a year later, with Salviati's support, they established a nearby design school affiliated with the new museum. There, using the antique pieces as examples, young apprentices would soon be encouraged to emulate the production of their glassmaking forebears. A period of intensive research and experimentation followed that culminated not only in the recovery of all the techniques used in the production of antique Murano glass but those of the ancient world as well.

The ramifications of Salviati's exposure to Lorenzo Radi's re-creations of antique Venetian glass resulted in nothing less than the revitalization of the entire Murano blown-glass industry and soon the historic island was infused with new artistic and economic life. Radi's work with chalcedony glass and especially the excitement it generated inspired Salviati's "Grand Vision"—a dream of once again firing up the furnaces of Murano and drawing out superb examples of the glassblower's art to be sold to connoisseurs and collectors in fine shops not only in Venice but throughout the world.

Salviati and the British

The time for bold economic expansion arrived in 1866 when, after nearly seventy years of foreign domination, Venice became part of the newly united Kingdom of Italy and was finally free. Salviati fervently believed that the revival of glass manufacture on Murano would be a great financial success. However, extensive capital investment was required. Radi's glass furnace in Venice was far too small to enable Salviati to realize his dream. New and larger furnaces would have to be laid down, glassblowers hired and trained, shops opened and staffed. Soon after locating and securing an available and suitably large exist-

Left to right: Francesco Ferro e Figlio. CHALCEDONY VASE. 1880–1900. H. 15⅜". Salviati Dott. Antonio fu Bartolomeo. Lorenzo Radi, maker. CHALCEDONY VASE. 1859–66. H. 5¾". Francesco Ferro e Figlio. CHALCEDONY EWER. 1880–1900. H. 13". Collection Gardner & Barr, New York

ing furnace at the impressive Gothic palazzo Da Mula[7] on Murano and lacking sufficient resources of his own to properly fire it up, Salviati had a brilliant idea.

Capitalizing on Britain's infatuation with Venice and on his own already impressive reputation there, Salviati went to London seeking financial backing. He knew Britain would be the ideal source for the capital investment he needed. The romantic nineteenth-century British were well known for their love of Venice, an island nation like their own, but recently fallen on hard times. Popular author John Ruskin had written *The Stones of Venice* in the early 1850s. This much-loved romanticized treatise on Venetian Gothic architecture became de rigueur reading for every British tourist visiting Venice on the Grand Tour. In it Ruskin unequivocally declared the idiosyncratic glass of Venice to be vastly superior to the overworked English cut crystal then being produced.[8] Shrewdly, Salviati realized that Ruskin had inadvertently created a market for evocative re-creations of antique Venetian glass that could be sold to the legions of wealthy British, Continental, and American tourists pouring into Venice. The courageous Dottore seized his moment.

In London, Salviati approached Sir Austen Henry Layard for capital investment. Layard was a wealthy and cultivated Englishman—a traveler, an art collector, and a member of Parliament. By no means a dilettante, he was the renowned archaeologist who had discovered and excavated the ruins of Nineveh in Assyria. More importantly for Salviati, he was an unabashed lover of Venice. He, and other similarly inclined Englishmen, including the historian William Drake, became Salviati's backers and partners.

The Società Anonima per azioni Salviati & C.

With financing secured, Salviati and his new British partners established the Società Anonima per azioni Salviati & C. on December 21, 1866. The company, based in London, had its factory on Murano at the palazzo Da Mula, which the new company purchased. In a short time Antonio Camozzo, a master glass technician, was busily at work laying down new furnaces at the palazzo. The production of both blown glass and mosaics would continue, but on a much larger scale. The showroom in Venice would continue to remain at Dorsoduro 731.

Salviati had been scouring Venice and Murano to find and employ the best glassblowers, designers, and technicians available even before the new company was formed. After years of economic depression this was no easy task. Fortunately, the glassmaker's craft was merely sleeping, not dead. Acting quickly, Salviati was able to recruit Antonio Seguso as his master foreman, and blowers Giovanni Serena and the Barovier brothers, Giovanni and Antonio, in less than a year. Perpetuating an unbroken tradition, he hired Angelo Ongaro, the last survivor of the famous glassblowing family. Ongaro was familiar with the nearly forgotten technique used to create filigree glass. In this way Salviati united under one roof the finest of Murano's surviving glassblowers, much to the delight of the Abbot Zanetti. Within the year Salviati secured the services of technicians Vincenzo Moretti and Luigi dalla Venezia.

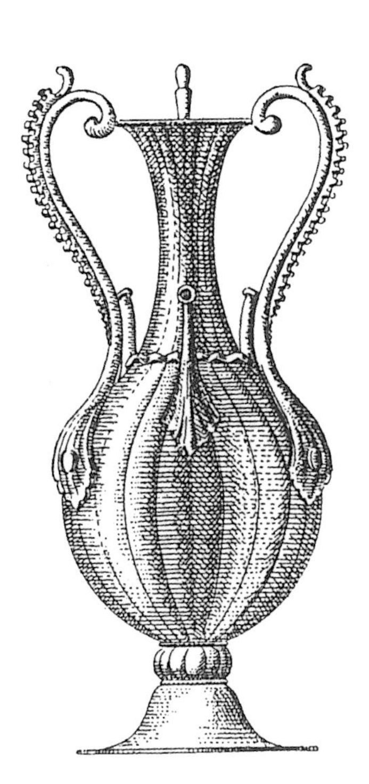

Years earlier, the young Moretti had started out in the simplest of menial jobs as a glass cane puller at the Pietro Bigaglia bead factory. Intrigued and inspired by the colors of the glass canes used in the manufacture of beads, a traditional Muranese industry that had survived (ironically because of Austria's need for colonial trading beads), Moretti began experimenting with glass on his own. Moretti and dalla Venezia took over the production of mosaic tesserae from Lorenzo Radi. Their combined talents earned a gold medal for the new firm at the Second Exhibition of Murano Glass in Venice in 1869, and it soon became the leading producer of mosaic tesserae, stocking over twenty-five hundred different colors. Salviati's new partner, archaeologist Layard, was passionately interested in recreating ancient glass. He spent a great deal of time at the glassworks working closely with Moretti, dalla Venezia, and Andrea Rioda, another talented young glassworker employed there. It was not surprising that years later, when Salviati and his British partners separated, the three technicians stayed with the British.

Few glassblowing talents of the caliber of Ongaro, the Baroviers, and Segusos could be found. These experienced glassblowers were expected to train the young, often illiterate, apprentices with whom Salviati was obliged to fill out the ranks of his new glassworks. Soon the Baroviers were joined by Antonio's three young sons, Benvenuto, Benedetto, and Giuseppe, who was only thirteen when he began work. Later, young Isidoro Seguso and Andrea Rioda joined in. Salviati earnestly believed that these young men could become the fine quality craftsmen he needed. He mandated their attendance at classes at the design school which he and Abbot Zanetti founded in 1862. There the young workers were shown

Glassblowers at the Salviati furnace, c. 1877. From a late nineteenth-century Salviati promotional booklet
The traditional Murano furnace was operated by one master glassblower surrounded by several helpers. The helpers, usually young apprentices, would often go on to become masters themselves. Salviati's glassworks had several furnaces.

examples of ancient Roman, Near Eastern, and antique Murano glass from the glass museum's growing study collection. Salviati and Zanetti hoped to motivate the young apprentices to equal and even excel the refined production of their glassmaking ancestors. At once obvious, Salviati's assault on these young minds was also subtle. Believing that literacy would improve their self-esteem and awaken pride in the great glassmaking heritage to which they were heir, he established a free school where the young men could learn to read and write.

While serving under Ongaro, Seguso, and the Barovier brothers the apprentices observed the complex techniques needed to replicate the antique glassware they had been shown at Murano's museum and design school. Ongaro was able to pass on the secrets needed to create filigree glass, a Venetian glassmaking technique that was invented in the sixteenth century by Filippo and Bernardo Catani.

Filigree falls into two distinct types. Its simplest form, *vetro a retorti* (twisted filigree), is produced by softening canes of glass incorporating twisted spirals of *lattimo* (milk) glass on a marble slab, a marver. Then a layer of softened glass known as the *pelle* (skin) is placed over the softened filigree canes and fused to them.[9] The resulting mass is returned to the furnace several times and blown into the desired shape. Although the Catanis were granted exclusive rights to the production of filigree for ten years by the Venetian Republic, in no time the revolutionary technique was copied by other European glassworks outside Venice.

The second, more complex form of filigree, its origin also dating to sixteenth-century Venice, is known as *vetro a reticello* (network filigree). In this complex technique a simple bubble with applied glass threading is inserted into another similar bubble with its applied threads arranged in the opposite direction. Carefully, one bubble is inserted into the other and the two are blown out together. The two bubbles fuse into a single object with a criss-cross pattern of threads. Interestingly, tiny bubbles of air are inadvertently trapped between the layers of glass in a regular pattern. By the seventeenth century both types of filigree had been elaborated by the use of ever more complex twisted canes and the addition of color.

By the early nineteenth century filigree glass had fallen into disuse. In 1830 Antonio Sanquirico, a Venetian antiques dealer commissioned the Ongaro family of glassmakers to copy some pieces of eighteenth-century blown filigree glass he owned. Ironically, it had been the Hapsburg Empire's need for glass trading beads that kept glassmakers utilizing, at small factories in Venice or at home, techniques such as filigree that would prove essential to the the revival of Murano's glass industry. After much trial and error the Ongaros succeeded in reproducing blown filigree glass for Sanquirico. They succeeded so well that the pieces were sold as antique by the less than scrupulous Sanquirico. While the pieces the Ongaros produced have long since vanished, Saniquirico's name has come down to us in the slightly corrupted form *zanfirico,* the generic Venetian term for filigree glass today.

The young glassblowers at Salviati quickly mastered the filigree techniques as well as many other newly rediscovered forgotten techniques. When they began blowing glass themselves, Salviati encouraged them to compete among themselves to produce the finest glass possible. His scheme paid off.

Proud of his accomplishment and never one to waste time, Salviati presented the palazzo Da Mula's initial production at the Paris Exposition of 1867, just one year after the furnace was fired up. He continued his award-winning tradition. Some idea of the rich and diversified range of the new production can be gained from illustrations in *The Art*

Societa Anonima per azioni Salviati & C. VETRO A RETICELLO TAZZA. 1866–70. H. 5¾".
Victoria and Albert Museum, London. Purchased from Salviati (73–1870)

Opposite: Societa Anonima per azioni Salviati & C. VETRO A RETORTI DECANTER.
1866–72. H. 14". Collection Gardner & Barr, New York

Glass production of the Societa Anonima per azioni Salviati & C., shown at the Paris International Exhibition of 1867

As evidenced by these illustrations, the glass produced by Salviati and Layard's new company for the 1867 Paris exhibition was heavily influenced by the antique Murano glass collected by Abbot Zanetti and Mayor Colleoni for Murano's study museum and its affiliated school. However, the distinctive nineteenth-century flavor of the fantasy glass that was to be the hallmark of Salviati's later production is already obvious in the fanciful serpents and technical bravura.

Journal Catalog of the Universal Exhibition and from Abbot Zanetti's ebullient description of the Salviati contribution: "Glasses, chalices, amphoras, cruets, vases, delicately tinted vessels harmonious with combinations of filigree and reticello, bands of enamel graffito, dazzling with aventurine, ruby, aquamarine, and opal, with borders, flowers, butterflies, serpents, dolphins, swans, initials, masks. . . ."[10] The firm was honored for the splendid colors of its filigree glass and the refined technique achieved in the application of glass threading to vases. The Salviati price lists of the period provide an interesting insight. The price of an object was dependent on the relative complexity of its production and color. For example, the range of prices began at the low end for an object executed in monochrome glass continued up in cost for multicolored glass and *vetro a retorti,* and finished at the highest end for glass executed in *vetro a reticello.*

The firm soon outgrew its small London shop and new, larger quarters were opened at 30 St James's Street in 1868. A year later, at Venice's Second Glass Exhibition the firm's newly developed "graffito" (now called "fenicio"[11]) glass was acclaimed in *La Voce di Murano* (The Voice of Murano).[12] Fenicio was produced by horizontally applying variously colored parallel glass threads to the body of a vase. The threads, while still soft, were combed, using a special tool, into festoons. The technique, which would be elaborated later by Vincenzo Moretti to produce so-called Phoenician glass, was derived from the pre-Roman glass of Phoenicia. Salviati also exhibited a selection of enameled glass at the 1869 exhibition, and Leopoldo Bearzotti is mentioned in contemporary reviews as the enamel painter of the Salviati shop. He exhibited Islamic-style enameled mosque lamps made for the viceroy of Egypt and enameled vases in the Etruscan style, but most of his enameled glass was derived from fifteenth- and early sixteenth-century pieces in the Murano museum's collection. Occasionally, fifteenth-century forms were enameled with distinctly eighteenth-century designs. In 1870 Antonio Seguso produced a copy of the well-known fifteenth-century enameled "coppa Barovier." (The original is still preserved in the Murano museum.) The Salviati glassworks was also producing fine quality *lattimo* vases, opaque white milk glass with enameled decoration imitating porcelain, ever more elaborate and colorful filigree glass, and opalescent vases decorated with aventurine threading. Aventurine is a type of glass in which tiny, metallic bits of copper appear in the body of the glass as it cools. The name derives from the Italian word for *accidental,* for indeed this glass was discovered serendipitously in the

Left to right: The Venice and Murano Glass Company Limited (Salviati & C.)/Salviati Dott. Antonio. GOURD VASE. 1872–95. H. 6¾". WINE GOBLET. 1872–95. H. 6⅛". Collection Gardner & Barr, New York
Morise, *small crests, are used to decorate these two blown aventurine glass objects. The crests are produced with small pliers that glassmakers use to pinch the still soft applied decoration into a serrated pattern.*

late seventeenth century. Initially it was produced in large lumps that were cut into small pieces for inlaid jewelry and small boxes. By the late eighteenth century the formula for aventurine glass had been forgotten and none was produced until Pietro Bigaglia rediscovered the complex recipe in the mid-nineteenth century. One obstacle remained, however: aventurine glass could not be blown. Challenged, the technicians at the Salviati furnaces overcame the difficulties and blown aventurine was introduced at the Trieste fair of 1871. Reputedly reserved for royal patrons, and perhaps it was at first, this elegant glass was nevertheless always difficult to produce and always expensive.

The revival of the Murano glass industry was now at full gallop. Production was dominated by Salviati's firm and the firm of Fratelli Toso which, having started up in 1854 manufacturing poor quality commercial glassware, soon rivaled Salviati in the production of top quality artistic glass. Like Salviati, the Fratelli Toso were awarded gold medals at the First and Second Glass Exhibitions in Murano in 1864 and 1869. The production of the two companies was very similar, with both working in the style known as *Vecchia Murano,* copies of antique Murano forms and techniques. Although ostensibly the aim of both houses was the faithful reproduction of examples from previous centuries, neither proved successful in suppressing the exuberant creativity of their young glassblowers who, ironically, were encouraged to exceed the creations of their ancestors in technical proficiency, contrary to both companies' publicly stated goal of historical accuracy.

In 1872, perhaps reflecting the growing animosity between Salviati and his British partners, the name of the company was anglicized to the Venice and Murano Glass and Mosaic Company Limited (Salviati & C.), but it remained popularly known as Compagnia di Venezia e Murano, and its success continued. Abandoning the small quarters at Dorsoduro 731, they bought the magnificent Renaissance palazzo Barbarigo on the Grand Canal and redesigned it to become the company's new Venetian headquarters. The facade was embellished with the firm's own mosaics depicting, among other events, the celebrated visit of French King Henri III to Murano in 1574.

Salviati continued garnering gold medals at the great industrial fairs that proliferated at the end of the nineteenth century. The publicity generated by these international events brought a steady flow of customers to the new showrooms. In 1873 Salviati and his employees triumphed at the Vienna International Exhibition. No less than thirteen Salviati glassmakers were awarded medals. Giovanni Barovier and his young nephew, Giuseppe, were singled out for their superb blown-glass creations. Vincenzo Moretti won for his mosaic tesserae. The Salviati firm itself received a prestigious *Diplome d'Honneur.*

In 1875 the eighteen-year-old Isidoro Seguso re-created the famous "Guggenheim cup" while at Salviati's glassworks. The elaborate seventeenth-century original was in the collection of Venetian antiques dealer Michelangelo Guggenheim. Taking up the challenge, Giuseppe Barovier, at twenty-three, also made a cup a year later. A great technical success, the cup was added to the Salviati catalogue, and probably, as examples were needed by the shop, was produced by both young glassblowers. The Salviati blowers continued challenging the limits of technique but the stylistic constraints of producing only historic revival glass was beginning to chafe the creative young men. Salviati was sympathetic.

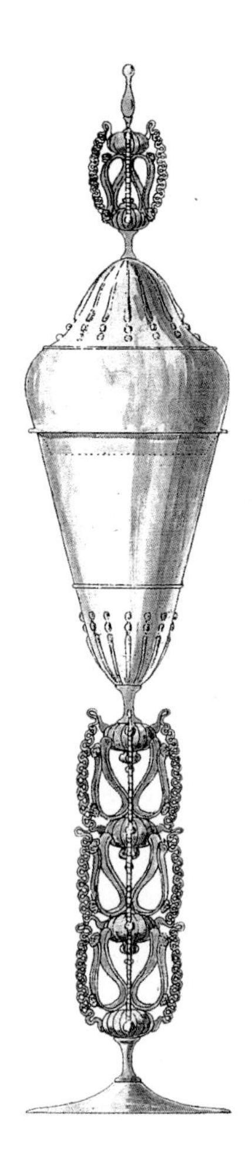

The Guggenheim vase as illustrated in the post-1877 Salviati Dott. Antonio glassworks catalogue. Collection Paolo Zancope, Venice

A Confusion of Names and Companies

There are many misconceptions surrounding Antonio Salviati and his businesses due in part to the numerous name changes. In fact, Salviati owned two types of factories on Murano, sometimes simultaneously, and he owned retail shops in Venice and London—all carrying the name Salviati. The first type of factory was devoted to mosaic production, Salviati's first business. There he created both finished mosaics for large-scale commissions or to sell in his shops and the raw material (mosaic tesserae) for sale to other mosaic manufacturers. His other factories, in which he sometimes had partners, were devoted to the production of blown glass. To add to the confusion, Salviati's shop sold the products of Salviati's various factories and those of other glassworks as well. The Salviati shops purchased glass from the Fratelli Toso furnaces, the Francesco Ferro e Figlio furnaces, and other smaller producers. It is therefore difficult to know, even if a piece is illustrated in one of the old Salviati & C. catalogues or has retained an old Salviati label, just who the actual manufacturer was. Some help is offered by studying the collection of the Murano Glass Museum, where the manufacturers donated examples of their work in the late nineteenth century and so the provenance of these gifts is recorded. To confuse matters more, the Salviati shops were not alone in selling glass in Venice. For instance, the Testolini shops purchased from the same sources as did Salviati, including, after 1883, the Salviati Dott.

Antonio glassworks itself. Many items in the Salviati Dott. Antonio glassworks catalogue appear in the post-1883 retail catalogues of both the Testolini and Salviati & C. shops. By 1895, many furnaces were producing traditional art glass for sale in the successful shops. Among the most prominent were Artisti Barovier (formerly Salviati Dott. Antonio), Fratelli Toso, Societa Operaja Arturo Nason & C. (the glassworks of the Testolini company after 1895), and Francesco Ferro & Figlio.

The individual glass craftsmen worked in almost total anonymity. True to the medieval craft guild tradition, the glassmakers regarded themselves as artisans, not artists. This attitude is reflected in the body of the work itself. No matter how loaded with ornament and nonfunctional an object became, it still ostensibly had a purpose. Only the glass factories themselves promoted their product as a whole. Occasionally an individual glassmaker would be singled out for a special honor at an international fair or Abbot Zanetti would mention him in his gossipy *Voice of Murano* newspaper. It was only in this way that we know, for example, that Vincenzo Moretti rediscovered murrhine glass or that Leopoldo Bearzotti produced enameled glass for Salviati. Individual artisans never signed anything and only very occasionally did a factory such as the Venice and Murano Glass & Mosaic Company Limited mark a piece with their logo. Paper labels were not meant to survive and most did not.

From the very first years of production it was widely but erroneously believed that Salviati's glassware was indistinguishable from the antique. In 1866 *The Art Journal* stated: "It is necessary to warn collectors that many of the modern productions of Salviati are selling as veritable antiques. Those who are not experienced connoisseurs may be easily deceived, for the imitations—or rather the copies—cannot be at once distinguished from the old. They are as light and as soft to the touch, the semi-transparency has been preserved, the colours are often as brilliant, and the designs are, in nearly all instances, after veritable models. Thus, the one can be scarcely distinguished from the other. . . ."[13] Clearly glass scholarship in the late nineteenth century had not progressed as quickly as had glass production. In 1881, the large collection of Murano glass given to New York's ten-year-old Metropolitan Museum of Art by James Jackson Jarves

Francesco Ferro e Figlio. DAPPLED EWER. H. 6". 1880–1900. Collection Gardner & Barr, New York
Inspired by ancient Roman glass in form, decoration, and technique, this macchie, *dappled or spotted, vessel was created by rolling a softened black glass cylinder over a marver strewn with softened multicolored opaque glass fragments that adhered to its surface. Several visits to the furnace and repeated rolling on the marver between blowings were necessary to bring this ewer to life.*

(now known as the "Jarves Gift"), contained many contemporary pieces, at the time mistakenly catalogued as sixteenth- and seventeenth-century works.[14] In reality, the insuppressible creativity of the young Murano glassblowers produced glass that was quintessentially nineteenth century from the very outset. Although the shapes were certainly inspired by antique Muranese production and the blowers had all the rediscovered techniques at their disposal, the glass itself could never be mistaken for earlier production today. Murano's nineteenth-century glass artisans made extensive use of elaborate and difficult zoomorphic forms; exotic animals abounded, dolphins, dragons, seahorses, serpents—nothing was too difficult. They were provided with an expanded chromatic range by advances in glass chemistry; deeper blues, richer purples, brilliant reds, and, of course, they indulged their typically nineteenth-century taste for overembellishment.

Salviati vs. Layard

Despite their notable successes, long-standing disagreements between Salviati and his British partners had reached a critical level by 1877. Perhaps Salviati's production was considered by his partner Layard to be too compromised and no longer faithful to their original concept of re-creating the antique glass of Murano and the ancient world. Salviati, on the other hand, realized that his young glassblowers wanted to produce more fanciful glass that showcased their mastery of the art and he sensed a strong market for their creations. After reaching the decision to sever their business relationship, Salviati was bought out by Layard and his other British partners. In so doing the British kept the name Venice and Murano Glass and Mosaic Company Limited (but dropped Salviati's name), the palazzo Da Mula glassworks, and the elegant shop in the palazzo Barbarigo. In short order Salviati opened a new Murano glassblowing furnace he named Salviati Dott. Antonio, and his own mosaic-covered shop, the palazzo Salviati, on the Grand Canal, not far from the Compagnia headquarters. All the Baroviers stayed with Salviati. Shortly after firing up the new Salviati Dott. Antonio glassblowing furnace, Salviati established a new company for the production of mosaics, predictably named Salviati & C. There the mosaic tesserae would be produced under the supervision of the Baroviers instead of Moretti and Rioda, who had remained with Layard.

Salviati's new headquarters at S. Gregorio on the Grand Canal, c. 1878.
From a Salviati promotional catalogue

Seguso and Barovier: Two Masters of Glass

Although stylistically the new companies would soon go their separate ways, when they exhibited their production at the Italian section of the Paris Universal Exhibition of 1878, just a year after the separation, contemporary critics considered their displays too similar. This so-called similarity was probably due to the fact that the Segusos, now working for the Compagnia, and the Baroviers, now at the new Salviati Dott. Antonio glassworks, would each continue for a time to blow their traditional product. Furthermore, the Compagnia had kept all the stock on hand when buying out Salviati, including, one must assume, pieces created by Giuseppe Barovier himself. Nearly identical versions of a covered chalice acquired by the Victoria & Albert Museum years before were exhibited by the Compagnia and the Salviati Dott. Antonio glassworks at the Paris fair. Rosa Barovier Mentasti suggests that Giuseppe Barovier, who had remained with Salviati, created both.[15]

In addition to their virtually identical traditional blown-glass production both companies exhibited similar examples of a new technique which the technicians at the old glassworks (now split between the two new companies) had been diligently researching. A Roman antiquities collector, the jeweler Augusto Castellani, presented the Murano Glass Museum with fragments of ancient Alexandrian and Roman slumped glass in 1873, and in 1876 British glass scholar Alexander Nesbitt did the same. Salviati too obtained a few shards in Rome. This ancient glass has the appearance of what we know as millifiori (thousand flower) glass. The techniques needed to produce this glass had been forgotten for nearly two thousand years. Stimulated and encouraged by the climate in the glassworks, which had always been one of constant experimentation, the Salviati glassmasters took up the challenge to re-create this intriguing nonblown glass. Vincenzo Moretti and his collaborators succeeded in rediscovering the lost processes just as Salviati and the British were separating.

The discovery that fragments of glass of different colors could be assembled and melted together to form attractive, multicolored glass objects was made by the earliest glass craftsmen. Eventually they learned to produce canes that were composed of glass of two or more colors arranged in patterns and fused together. These thick canes would then be heated until soft and then pulled out by two cane pullers until a long thin rod was formed. This

Exhibited at the Paris Universal Exhibition of 1878 by both Salviati Dott. Antonio and the Venice and Murano Glass Company Limited, this line drawing is taken from the post-1883 Testolini shop's retail sales catalogue

Societa Anonima per azioni Salviati & C. COVERED CHALICE. 1866–70. H. 21¼". Victoria and Albert Museum, London (82–1870)
Acquired by the South Kensington Museum (now the V&A) in 1870, this model was kept in production for many years. The design is based on seventeenth-century Bohemian prototypes. Another example is in the Corning Museum of Glass, Corning, New York.

The Venice and Murano Glass Company Limited. Vincenzo Moretti, maker. MURRHINE GLASS VASE. 1878. H. 4¾", Diam. 4⅞". Mark: murrhine bearing initial V superimposed over initial M. The Metropolitan Museum of Art, New York. Gift of James Jackson Jarves, 1881 (81.8.31) (shown actual size)

rod, when sliced into roundels like a cucumber, produced murrhine—disks of colored glass that exhibit identical and often intricate patterns.

Murrhine can be utilized in glass production in two ways. Glass produced by the first technique is called *murrhine glass.* Moretti was responsible for retrieiving this ancient technique. The ancient glassmakers arranged their murrhine on a slab of marble, the marver, closely packed side to side. The marver was then put into the furnace and heated slowly until the murrhine disks melted and fused together. The resulting molten mass was picked up and slumped, draped over or into a simple form, usually plate or cup shaped. After cooling, the resulting dish or cup was polished to reveal the intricate and colorful patterns of the now fused murrhine. The second technique results in *mosaic glass,* formerly called millifiori.[16] It was invented in the sixteenth century in an attempt to imitate ancient slumped glass by blowing. Even then the slumping technique had been forgotten for centuries. Starting off in the same way, murrhine are arranged side by side on a marver and heated until soft. Then a layer of softened glass, the skin, is placed, or rolled, over the murrhine and fused to them. The resulting mass, murrhine on the outside, clear or colored glass on the inside, is manipulated into a bubble and then blown into the desired shape.

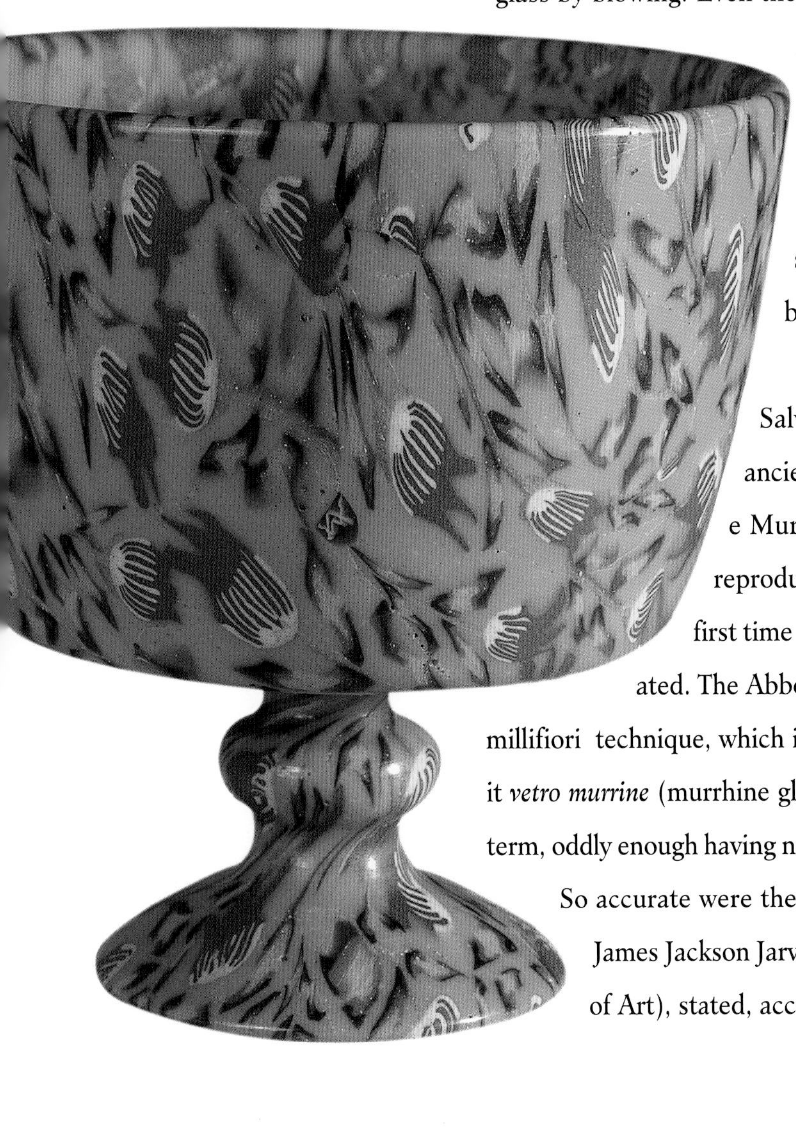

When the two new companies were formed Moretti left Salviati's employ and began to produce his reproductions of ancient murrhine glass for the British. The Compagnia di Venezia e Murano chose the 1878 Paris exhibition to introduce Moretti's reproductions and they attracted exuberant critical acclaim. For the first time since antiquity, ancient slumped murrhine glass had been created. The Abbot Zanetti, to distinguish this new glass from the Renaissance millifiori technique, which imitated ancient glass by blowing, wasted no time in dubbing it *vetro murrine* (murrhine glass). He derived the name murrhine from an ancient Roman term, oddly enough having nothing to do with glass but referring to a semiprecious stone.[17] So accurate were these re-creations that Alexander Nesbitt, when shown one by James Jackson Jarves (and presumably now in New York's Metropolitan Museum of Art), stated, according to Jarves, "if a fragment of it had been brought to him in Rome, he would have sworn it was ancient glass."[18] At the Paris exhibition Moretti's new murrhine glass was wildly successful. All forty-six pieces exhibited were sold, "purchased for handsome sums by the most eminent persons. . . ."[19]

The superiority of the blown mosaic glass technique vs. the slumped murrhine glass is easy to see. The shapes possible with the latter are severely limited, as is the size and thickness of the finished product. Using the mosaic glass technique, the range of shapes and sizes is limitless as the glass may be blown to any thickness, or more correctly *thinness,* desired by the glassmaker.

The younger Baroviers, Giuseppe and Benvenuto, preferred the mosaic glass technique. They had exhibited examples in 1871 at both the Maritime Exhibition in Naples and the Trieste Exhibition and later at Milan's 1881 exhibition. The quality of their production is superb, the skin is so thin that it virtually disappears, giving the illusion that the objects are made solely of fused murrhine, which they are not. Later, the firm of Fratelli Toso, between 1900 and 1914, produced a large quantity of vases in mosaic glass, including pieces with elaborate floral murrhine. What is arguably the most important piece of early mosaic glass to survive, truly heralding the Baroviers' future production, was presented to New York's Metropolitan Museum of Art by James Jackson Jarves in 1881 (see page 69). However, due to the time-consuming nature and difficulty of this technique and the resulting high price, production was relatively small and surviving pieces are rare. Salviati soon lost interest in producing this expensive glass and halted its production. The Barovier family, especially young Giuseppe, would never lose interest in mosaic glass and, keeping the technique in reserve, were destined to produce superb examples in the early decades of the twentieth century.

Separate Ways

As it happens, in 1877 the two most important and successful Venetian glass companies were born out of a disagreement between Salviati and Layard. Each company, as we know, was to follow a different path. Vincenzo Moretti, the two Segusos, Antonio and Isidoro, Giovanni Serena, and Andrea Rioda stayed with the now British-owned Compagnia. Under Layard's exclusive direction the Compagnia soon dedicated itself to the strict reproduc-

Andrea Rioda & C.
Andrea Rioda, designer.
GOBLET. 1911–21. H. 7⅛". Diam. 5¼". Collection Gardner & Barr, New York
Rioda took over the Palazzo da Mula glass furnace when The Venice and Murano Glass Company closed in 1910. He would continue the production of traditional antique-style glass for ten years.

tion of ancient glass. Moretti supplied its two Venetian shops with murrhine glass.[20] Encouraged by Layard, he continued his experiments in the reproduction of other types of ancient glass. In 1881 at the National Exhibition in Milan, Moretti's new creation *vetro fenici* ("Phoenician" glass) was introduced. These vases of variously colored festoons of glass "combed" over a solid colored surface were perfect replicas of pre-Roman Mesopotamian, Egyptian, and Phoenician glass, similar to pieces seen by Layard in the Near East while conducting his excavations at Nineveh. While the ancient pieces were created by the time-consuming method of core forming,[21] these accurate duplicates were created by blowing. Strangely, Layard seems to have been more interested in the appearance of the finished "Phoenician" pieces than in the unorthodox method used to produce them. Perhaps he was finally acquiescing to the exigencies of commerce—efficient and quick production. Layard's continued preoccupation with the strict reproduction of ancient Roman glass was evidenced by the production of a line of black glass vases and ewers, sometimes slightly iridescent, decorated with colorful linear applications, usually a bright yellow, and a series of reproductions of flat panes of gold-leafed paleo-Christian glass. The Compagnia's commercially unsuccessful attempt at re-creating Roman cameo glass was due to the efforts of Attilia Spaccarelli of Rome. Andrea Rioda became technical manager in 1901, but the firm closed its palazzo Da Mula factory in 1910. A year later the magnificent shop on the Grand Canal was taken over by the Testolini company. For ten years, beginning in 1911, Rioda kept the old glassworks producing under his own name, Andrea Rioda & C. There, surrounded by the craftsmen of the old Compagnia furnace, he continued producing traditional antique-style glass.

Dolphins and Dragons

Giovanni Barovier and his nephews Giuseppe, Benvenuto, and Benedetto remained with Salviati as his master glassblowers at the new Salviati Dott. Antonio glassworks. There they specialized in a loose interpretation of Venetian blown glass of the sixteenth, seventeenth, and eighteenth centuries. Not content with the mere slavish copying of old pieces, and encouraged by Salviati, they competed among themselves and succeeded not only in out-

Opposite: Salviati Dott. Antonio/Artisti Barovier. Giuseppe Barovier, maker. DRAGON COMPOTE. 1877–1914. H.11½", Diam. 11¼". Collection Marjorie Reed Gordon, New York
Executed in the granzioli *technique, which was perfected by the Baroviers, the entire surface of this compote is covered with raised bits of turquoise glass.*

Below: A closeup of the dragon compote

doing their ancestors but each other as well. Between the years 1877 and 1914, in this fertile atmosphere of cooperative competition, the Barovier family, with unbridled imagination, created ever more elaborate, more fantastically colored, technically flawless examples of late nineteenth- and early twentieth-century Murano glass. Just as Venice's architecture is infused with the combined traditions of ancient Rome and the exotic East, so too the glassware of the Baroviers exhibits a hybrid iconography that never fails to amaze. Embellished with ancient and medieval mythological animals, Murano's glassware brought the beastiary of the ancient world and the Middle Ages to the door of the twentieth century. Surprisingly, the lion of St. Mark and the crocodile of St. Theodore (Venice's first patron saint) are virtually unknown in Murano's menagerie. Dolphins and dragons, storks and swans, seahorses, hippocamps, serpents, and winged horses, are not.

In the panoply of decorative motifs used by Murano's glassmakers the dragon takes pride of place. This preoccupation with dragons harks back to Near Eastern mythology of the Middle Ages. Although dragons were not commonly used in the sixteenth- and seventeenth-century glass of Murano, the motif can be found in Renaissance rock crystal and metal objects and in period paintings. Originating in ancient China, the dragon slithered westward through the arts of Persia and Byzantium, finding its final refuge in the glassware of Murano.

The dragon's close challenger for first place is the ubiquitous dolphin. An ancient symbol of immortality, the dolphin is well known to us from the famed Greek and Roman "boy on a dolphin" legend. Real dolphins also abound in the waters of the Mediterranean and were undoubtedly a familiar sight to Venetian seamen.

Seeking to create ever more elaborate, technically challenging glassware, the late nineteenth-century Murano glassblowers, especially the Barovier brothers, Giuseppe and Benvenuto, concocted ever more complicated and bizarre

Artisti Barovier or Fratelli Toso. DRAGON PITCHER. 1895–1914. H. 11". Collection Marjorie Reed Gordon, New York

zoomorphic combinations, dragons fighting serpents, dolphins supporting shells supporting winged horses, and so on. Salviati's former partner Layard probably hated these flights of fantasy, but the world loved them.

As a relief from these complicated creations the Baroviers simultaneously blew a series of thin-walled, straw-colored vases distinctly inspired by, but not copied from, sixteenth-century Venetian examples. For a short time they produced another series of vases dubbed *corinto* (Corinthian). These vases were unconvincing re-creations of pitted, corroded ancient pieces being excavated in Corinth, but, more significantly, they represented a philosophical departure by the Salviati firm. Layard would have preferred to re-create the ancient pieces exactly as they looked when new. These pieces, first produced by the Baroviers and then, between 1880 and 1900, by Francesco Ferro & Figlio, relied on bits of multicolored glass and/or gold and silver leaf to suggest the corroded surface of long-buried ancient glass.

Before long, and with Salviati's approval, the Baroviers decided to launch their own business Fratelli Barovier in 1878. The firm consisted of ten glassmaster partners, including all the Baroviers, Camozzo, and Antonio Seguso, who had returned to the Salviati fold. They worked out of the Salviati Dott. Antonio glasshouse on Murano and maintained a close contractual relationship with Salviati, producing a good deal of glass exclusively for the Salviati & C. shops. These exclusive items consisted of items already in the Salviati & C. catalogue and items for which Salviati himself had provided designs. Glass not reserved for Salviati could be sold to other Venetian retail shops and the Testolini & C. shop became an important customer. In 1883, at age sixty-seven, Salviati transferred the ownership of the factory to the Barovier family. A year after Salviati's death in 1890 the Baroviers enlarged the glass factory and even set up an exhibition furnace in London for six months. However, by previous agreement with Salviati the name Salviati Dott. Antonio was kept until 1895 when it was finally changed to Artisti Barovier. With this expansion several changes were instituted in production techniques. An alternate method of coloring glass was extensively used. Instead of preparing a batch of glass for each individual color, the colorless nascent creation attached to the blow pipe would be rolled over a marver strewn with tiny bits of pulverized colored glass that would adhere to its surface. After further blowing and smoothing on the marver the object would be covered by tiny dots of color. This process, while not at all compromising quality, provided for quicker and cheaper pro-

Artisti Barovier or Fratelli Toso. RED DRAGON VASE. 1900–1914. H. 14" Collection Marjorie Reed Gordon, New York

duction. The introduction of a new color to the glassmaker's repertoire, a bright blood red,[22] a more extensive use of fragmented gold leaf spread over the surface, and the occasional use of iridescence added new dimensions to the still predominantly traditional production of the Barovier family.

Success Brings Stagnation

Dedicated to satisfying the demanding Venetian shops, the glassworks of Murano in the late nineteenth and early twentieth centuries were content to continue producing glass more or less directly copied from that of their ancestors or elaborate, hybrid nineteenth-century tours de force. They ignored the trends that were taking place in Europe and America where the newly discovered arts of Japan were creating an aesthetic awareness that would soon culminate in the birth of Art Nouveau. This myopic point of view was encouraged by the large shops, which, catering almost exclusively to the wealthy tourist trade, were unwilling to tamper with what was for them a great merchandising success.

After Salviati's death in 1890, his son Giulio took over the management of the firm along with Maurizio Camerino, a trusted employee, as his new partner. In 1897 they opened a large new shop in London called Salviati Jesurum & C., at 235–241 Regent Street, which was actually an association of several large Venetian shops selling fabrics as well as glass.[23] The shop survived for ten years, until 1907. The elaborate mosaic decoration of the facade survives today and, intriguingly, advertises branches in Paris, New York, St. Petersburg, and Berlin. When Giulio died in 1898 Maurizio Camerino became sole owner of all the shops but wisely kept the name Salviati & C. He continued selling glass produced by the Baroviers, but, as always, patronized the other major glass factories of Murano. Antonio Salviati's surviving son Silvio joined with Camerino in 1903 in a new venture they named Erede Dott. A. Salviati & Co. which opened for business just next to the palazzo Salviati on the Grand Canal. The traditional blown-glass fantasies sold there were in some cases identical to those sold in the Venetian and London shops owned by Camerino, so obviously the two closely related companies patronized the same glasshouses, predominantly the Artisti Barovier.

In 1895 the First Venice International Art Exhibition, the Biennale, was scheduled to

Fratelli Toso. PHOENICIAN-STYLE VASE. 1900–1914. H. 6⅛". Collection Gardner & Barr, New York
The re-creation of ancient Near Eastern core-formed glass was perfected by Vincenzo Moretti in 1881. The Fratelli Toso, utilizing Moretti's techniques, blew a series of these vases in the years 1900 to 1914. (shown actual size)

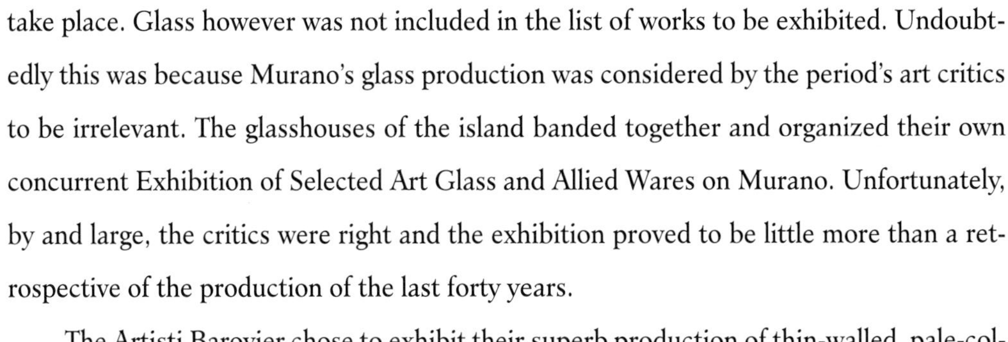

take place. Glass however was not included in the list of works to be exhibited. Undoubtedly this was because Murano's glass production was considered by the period's art critics to be irrelevant. The glasshouses of the island banded together and organized their own concurrent Exhibition of Selected Art Glass and Allied Wares on Murano. Unfortunately, by and large, the critics were right and the exhibition proved to be little more than a retrospective of the production of the last forty years.

The Artisti Barovier chose to exhibit their superb production of thin-walled, pale-colored glass vases and goblets distinctly reminiscent of the work of sixteenth-century Muranese glassblowers. Stylistically similar to these but showing a distinct Art Nouveau influence, they presented three extremely fragile vases with spiral stems. With these three vases, and alone among all Murano's glasshouses, the Artisti Barovier demonstrated an avant-garde tendency almost unknown in Murano. Despite the fact that the majority of their production was still in the predominant *Vecchia Murano* style, they nevertheless, albeit in a small way, heralded the streamlined production of the twentieth century yet to come.

Ironically, Fratelli Toso, Murano's oldest surviving glass factory, came into its own during this difficult transitional period. In 1910 they introduced a new line of beautifully crafted vases and lamps. These objects were executed in the mosaic glass technique that, by 1871, the Baroviers had perfected for Salviati. Simultaneously, the company produced a series of festooned Phoenician-style vases similar to those Vincenzo Moretti produced for the Compagnia di Venezia e Murano in 1881 and "floreale" vases in which threads of glass imitating stems and leaves and elaborate flower-shaped murrhine were embedded in a solid color base. These new creations were a great success, both financially and aesthetically for the Fratelli Toso.

A New Challenge

Slowly, beginning in 1905, the conservative Venice Biennale opened its doors to foreign exhibitors. The city's artistic isolation had finally been breached. At the Biennale of 1910 two young Venetian artists, Teodoro Wolf-Ferrari and Vittorio Zecchin, marveled at the work of Austrian Secessionist painter Gustav Klimt. Inspired by Klimt's distinctive style they designed a series of thirteen objects that they wanted to produce in mosaic glass believing that lead joints, unavoidable in ordinary stained glass, would interfere with the painterly effect they desired. They approached their friend Giuseppe Barovier with their designs. Barovier and his brother Benvenuto had recently resurrected the complex mosaic glass technique which they had virtually abandoned in 1881 when Antonio Salviati lost interest in its production and sale. Giuseppe created Zecchin and Wolf-Ferrari's challenging objects at the Artisti Barovier furnace after the other glassblowers had left for the day. The pieces he created were exhibited by Zecchin and Wolf-Ferrari first at the Windhager Art Exhibition in Munich in 1913 and once again at the 11th Biennale in 1914. That same year, at a landmark exhibition, the *Fiera mostra dei fiori* (a flower show under the porticos of the doge's palace) the Artisti Barovier exhibited an award-winning mosaic glass production designed by the Barovier brothers themselves. Some of the pieces exhibited were identified with a small murrina bearing the initials AMF 1914.[24] These masterpieces were sold at the Salviati shops alongside the traditional Vecchia Murano glassware which the Artisti Barovier would continue to produce.

MOSAIC GLASS VASE
(detail of murrhine)

From 1914 to 1918, having entered World War I on the side of France and Britain, Italy found herself once again at war with Austria. Venice, practically on the front lines, was shelled by the Austro-German army. The glass factories Artisti Barovier, Fratelli Toso, and Andrea Rioda & C. fled Murano for Livorno. Understandably, Venice's all-important tourist industry came to a complete halt.

With the war over and Italy and her allies triumphant, a semblance of normalcy and tourists had returned to Venice by 1920. That year Maurizio Camerino once again become sole owner of all the shops bearing the Salviati name when Silvio Salviati retired, but he was facing two big problems. Not only had the market for Murano's traditional production declined even among Venice's loyal tourist trade, but Camerino's supply of glassware was threatened. Giuseppe Barovier, at sixty-seven, was no longer interested in producing traditional wares for the Venetian shops. He and his brother Benvenuto preferred to spend their remaining years crafting elaborate, unique, and expensive mosaic glass pieces. The younger generation of Baroviers, exploring new styles and techniques, had no interest in traditional production either. Another important supplier, Andrea Rioda, was preparing to cede his business in the palazzo Da Mula to a new company which was being formed by Giacomo Cappellin and Paolo Venini. Ironically, Rioda, who was to have been kept on as

Societa Anonima per azioni Salviati & C.
CHALCEDONY EWER.
1866–72. H. 8¾".
Collection Adriana Mnuchin, New York
The use of startling new color combinations, bits of aventurine glass, and, occasionally, fragments of filigree glass or murrhine added nineteenth-century drama to the production of chalcedony glass by Salviati's blowers.

technical director, died before the new company began production. Camerino, like Salviati before him, seized his moment. He joined with all of Rioda's former glassblowers and opened a new glass factory named Successori Andrea Rioda, which produced glass in the traditional manner, but with a simplified, almost Art Deco flavor, exclusively for the Salviati shops until 1938.

Slowly as Murano's old guard gave way to a new generation of glassmakers, a stylistic change swept over the island. After the First World War, the taste for the elaborate traditional glassware that had been the mainstay of the Venetian shops for decades gave way to a preference for a simpler, lighter, paler production. Obviously inspired by sixteenth-century prototypes, including vases and goblets seen in the Renaissance paintings of Veronese, Tintoretto, and Holbein, the Baroviers had been producing these unembellished vases at the Salviati Dott. Antonio glasshouse since 1878 and had featured them at Murano's Exhibition of Selected Art Glass and Allied Wares in 1895. It was not until the 1920s, however, that they caught the world's fancy. As the the worldwide rage for Art Deco gained strength in the late teens, the demand for Murano's streamlined glass grew stronger. The new Vetreria Artistica Barovier continued the simplified production pioneered by the Artisti Barovier, its predecessor, and the two new glasshouses, Successori Andrea Rioda and Cappellin Venini, began producing this pale, extremely light, blown glass.

From the Past to the Future

The Murano glass renaissance, drawing on historic references, led the island's glass industry and indeed the world's, into the modern epoch. During this sixty-year period the forgotten glassmaking techniques of two millennia were recovered and new methods of manipulating glass were invented and perfected. When, by the 1930s, the young glassmakers of Murano had at last joined the artistic quest the rest of the world had been pursuing for decades, they were armed with an unrivaled repertoire of technical expertise. Ever since at the forefront of art glass production, Murano's glassmasters have served as icons for aspiring glass artists. They have succeeded in passing on the centuries-old tradition of their ancestors and in so doing have ensured the survival of their craft in the centuries to come.

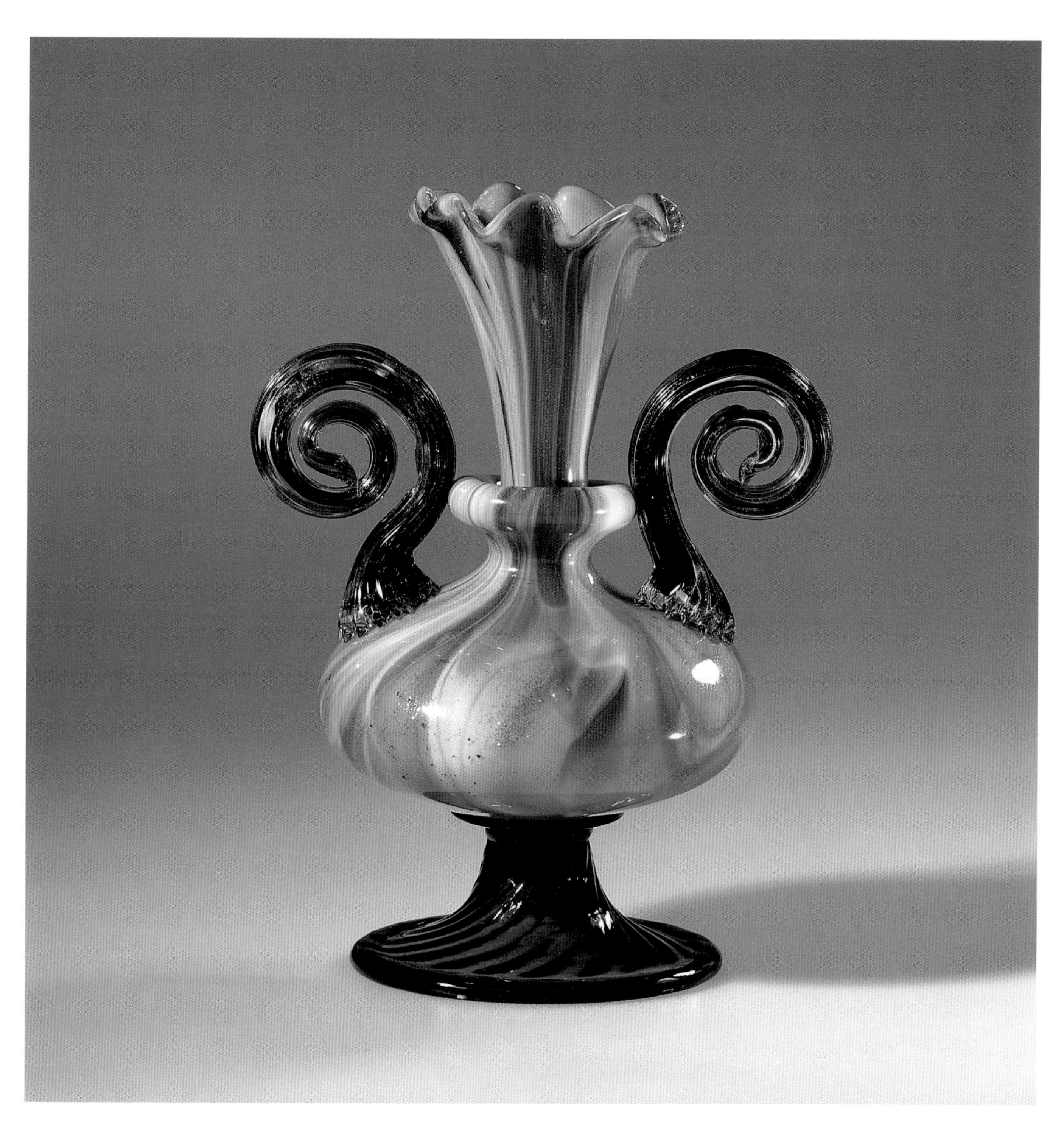

Societa Anonima per azioni Salviati & C. CHALCEDONY VASE. 1866–68. H. 7¾".
Victoria and Albert Museum, London. Purchased from Salviati in 1868 (896–1868)

Opposite: Societa Anonima per azioni Salviati & C. CHALCEDONY VASE. 1866–68. H. 12".
Victoria and Albert Museum, London. Purchased from Salviati in 1868 (894–1868)

Left to right: Societa Anonima per azioni Salviati & C. 1866–72. DECANTER. H. 8¾". Collection Gardner & Barr, New York. DECANTER. 1866–72. H. 13". Collection Adriana Mnuchin, New York

Opposite, clockwise, from top left: Societa Anonima per azioni Salviati & C. VETRO A FILI DECANTER WITH STOPPER. 1866–72. H. 15¾". VETRO A FILI AVENTURINE DECANTER WITH STOPPER. 1866–72. H. 11". DECANTER WITH BLUE RIGAREE. 1866–72. H. 9". STRAW-COLORED DECANTER. 1866–72. H. 9". DECANTER WITH APPLIED PRUNTS AND STOPPER. 1866–72. H. 10". Collection Marjorie Reed Gordon, New York

Societa Anonima per azioni Salviati & C. COVERED BOWL. 1866–72. H. 4¾".
Collection Robert Conant, New York (shown actual size)

Opposite, left to right: Societa Anonima per azioni Salviati & C. VETRO A FILI DECANTER.
1866–72. H. 10¾". Collection Marjorie Reed Gordon, New York.
PHOENICIAN-STYLE DECANTER. 1866–72. H. 12". Collection Gardner & Barr, New York

Societa Anonima per azioni Salviati & C. SERPENT STEM GOBLET. 1866. H.7¼".
Victoria and Albert Museum, London. Gift of Salviati & C., 1937 (C39–1937)

Opposite: Societa Anonima per azioni Salviati & C. VASE. 1866–68. H. 9⅞".
Victoria and Albert Museum, London. Purchased from Salviati in 1868 (905–1868)

Left to right: Societa Anonima per azioni Salviati & C. ENAMELED GOBLET. 1866–72. H. 4⅛", Diam. 3⅞". ENAMELED GOBLET. 1866–72. H. 4¼", Diam. 4¼". Collection Gardner & Barr, New York. ENAMELED CUP & SAUCER. 1866–72. H. 3", Diam. 5⅝". Collection Marjorie Reed Gordon, New York

Societa Anonima per azioni Salviati & C. PHOENICIAN-STYLE TAZZA. 1866–69. H. 6".
Victoria and Albert Museum, London. Purchased from Salviati (67–1870)

Societa Anonima per azioni Salviati & C.
ENAMELED GOBLET. 1866–72. H. 7⅞", Diam. 4¾".
The Metropolitan Museum of Art, New York.
Gift of James Jackson Jarves, 1881 (81.8.220)

Opposite: Societa Anonima per azioni Salviati & C.
Leopoldo Bearzotti, decorator (attribution).
ENAMELED CHALICE. 1866–72. H. 13⅞".
Collection Gardner & Barr, New York
The form and "fish scale" enameled decoration of this goblet are derived from late fifteenth- and early sixteenth-century examples. The coat of arms with papal attributes was probably a special order.

The Venice and Murano Glass Company Limited (Salviati & C.)/Salviati Dott. Antonio.
SCALLOP SHELL EWER. 1872–95. H. 8⅛", Diam. 3⅞". Collection Gardner & Barr, New York

Opposite: Salviati Dott. Antonio/Artisti Barovier. Giuseppe or Benvenuto Barovier, maker.
BLOWN AVENTURINE VASE. 1877–1914. H. 9⅞". Collection Gardner & Barr, New York
A rare example of a difficult and probably experimental technique attempting to imitate the pitted and corroded surface of ancient glass. In this vase the blown aventurine body is encased in a layer of bubbly, weblike clear glass.

The Venice and Murano Glass Company Limited. Vincenzo Moretti, maker.
MURRHINE GLASS VASE. 1878. H. 5½", Diam. 5". Mark: murrhine bearing initial
V superimposed over initial M. Collection Gardner & Barr, New York
These vases were frequently signed with a murrina *bearing the initials VM. Rather than representing the initials of Vincenzo Moretti, or even Vetro Murrine, VM is the logo of The Venice and Murano Glass Company Limited.*

Opposite: Detail of murrhine

Opposite, left to right: Fratelli Toso. MOSAIC GLASS PITCHER. 1900–1914. H. 5¾". The Venice and Murano Glass Company Limited (Salviati & C.)/Salviati Dott. Antonio. Giuseppe or Benvenuto Barovier, maker. MOSAIC GLASS PITCHER. 1872–95. H. 5½". Collection Gardner & Barr, New York

Right: MOSAIC GLASS PITCHER (details)

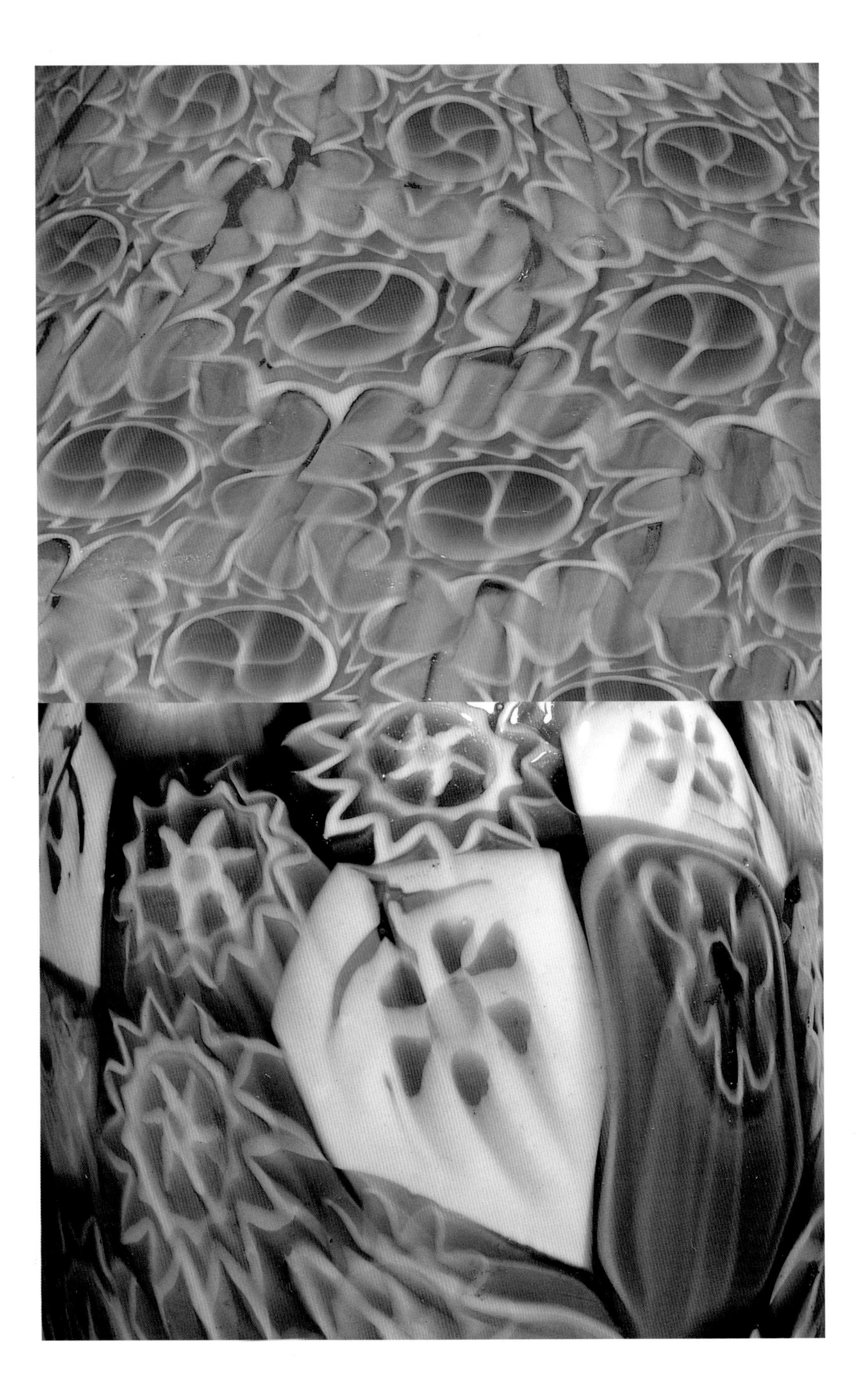

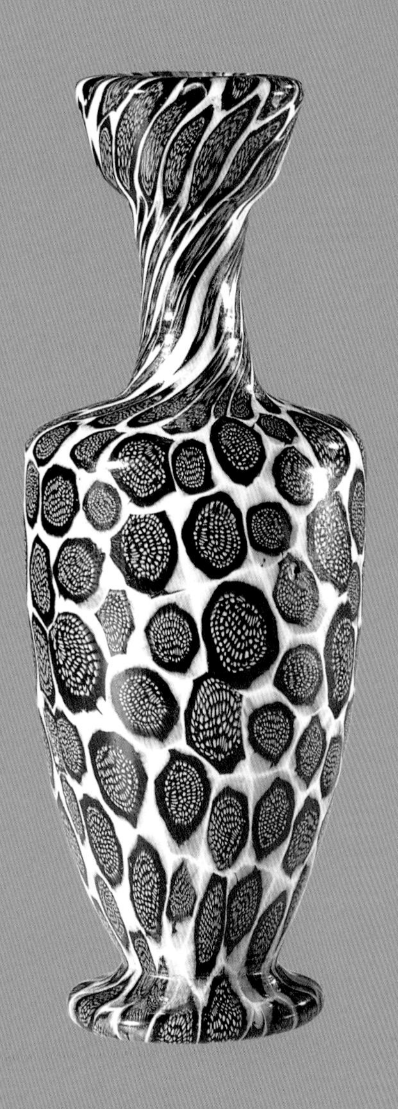

The Venice and Murano Glass Company Limited (Salviati & C.). Giuseppe or Benvenuto Barovier, maker. MOSAIC GLASS VASE. 1872. H. 5". Victoria and Albert Museum, London. Purchased from maker, 1873 (shown actual size)

Opposite: The Venice and Murano Glass Company Limited (Salviati & C.)/Salviati Dott. Antonio. Giuseppe or Benvenuto Barovier, maker. MOSAIC GLASS VASE WITH COVER. 1872–81. H. 12", Diam. 7". The Metropolitan Museum of Art, New York. Gift of James Jackson Jarves, 1881 (81.8.213ab)

The Venice and Murano Glass Company Limited. Ewer. 1881–1910. H. 6⅛". Collection Gardner & Barr, New York (shown actual size)

Opposite, left to right: The Venice and Murano Glass Company Limited. Vincenzo Moretti, designer/maker. Phoenician-style Pitcher. 1881–1910. H. 3⅞". Phoenician-style Vase. 1881–1910. H. 9". Phoenician-style Vase. 1881–1910. H. 5⅝". Phoenician-style Pitcher. 1881–1910. H. 6¼". Collection Gardner & Barr, New York

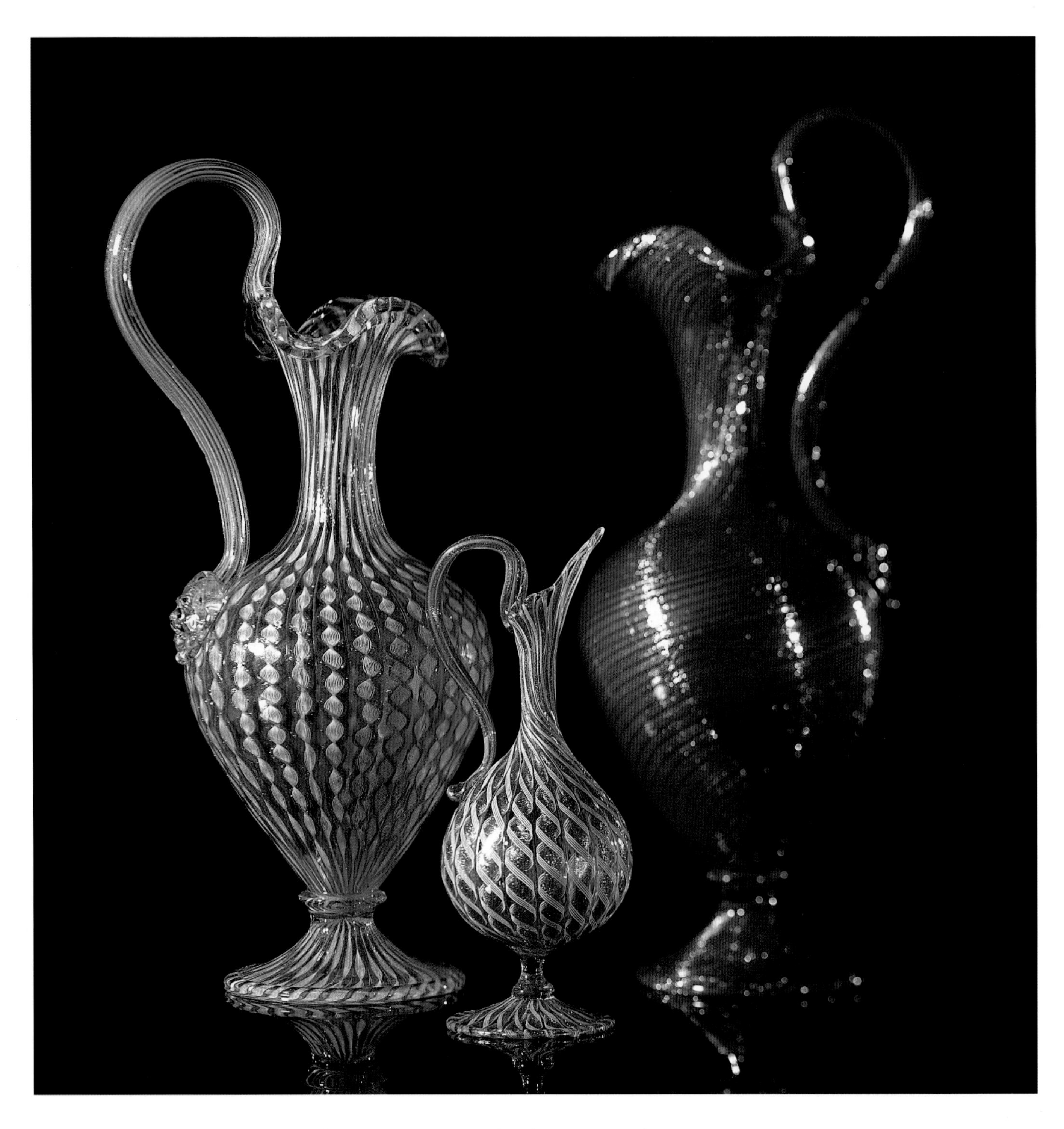

Left to right: The Venice and Murano Glass Company Limited (Salviati & C.)/Salviati Dott. Antonio. VETRO A RETORTI PITCHER. 1872–95. H. 13". VETRO A RETORTI PITCHER. 1872–95. H. 7¼". Collection Gardner & Barr, New York. VETRO A FILI AVENTURINE PITCHER. 1872–95. H. 13½". Collection Adriana Mnuchin, New York

Opposite: Salviati Dott. Antonio/Artisti Barovier. VETRO A FILI AVENTURINE FOOTED COMPOTE. 1877–1914. H. 7¼", Diam. 10⅝". Collection Gardner & Barr, New York

Left to right: The Venice and Murano Glass Company Limited (Salviati & C.)/Salviati Dott. Antonio. PUMPKIN-SHAPED BOWL. 1872–95. H. 4⅛", Diam. 7". OCTAGONAL BOWL. 1872–95. H. 2⅞", Diam. 4⅛". Collection Gardner & Barr, New York
These two bowls are executed in the technique known in Murano as screziato *which, simply translated, means "multicolored."*

Opposite, left to right: The Venice and Murano Glass Company Limited (Salviati & C.). YELLOW VASE. 1872–77. H. 7 ¼". YELLOW SCREZIATO (MULTICOLOR) VASE. 1872–77. H. 5¾". SCREZIATO (MULTICOLOR) VASE. 1872–77. H. 5¾". MARBLEIZED VASE. 1872–77. H. 5 ½". Collection Gardner & Barr, New York

Opposite, inset, left to right: Societa Anonima per azioni Salviati & C./The Venice and Murano Glass Company Limited (Salviati & C.)/Salviati Dott. Antonio or Artisti Barovier. PHOENICIAN-STYLE BEAKER. 1869–95. H. 3¼". VETRO A RETORTI BEAKER. 1867–95. H. 3⅛". BLOWN AVENTURINE BEAKER WITH TURQUOISE GRANZIOLI. 1871–1914. H. 3¾". VETRO A FILI BEAKER WITH APPLIED AVENTURINE THREADING AND PRUNTS. 1867–1914. H. 3¼". VETRO A RETICELLO BEAKER. 1867–1914. H. 3⅝". Collection Gardner & Barr, New York

Seen together, these five beakers provide a lexicon of late nineteenth century glassmaking techniques. Beginning left to right, the pink, white, and aventurine beaker is crafted in the technique originally called graffito, scraped, *but now generally known as* fenicio, or *Phoenician style. It was introduced by Salviati at Venice's Second Glass Exhibition in 1869. The next, in classic sixteenth-century style, is* vetro a retorti *and won critical acclaim for the Salviati firm when reintroduced at the 1867 Universal Exhibition in Paris. The center beaker is formed of blown aventurine glass, a new technique that was invented by the Salviati craftsmen and introduced at the Trieste Fair of 1871. Often, such blown aventurine objects were embellished with small bits of red, white, or turquoise glass in a method known as* granzioli. *The fourth beaker is decorated with aventurine prunts and applied aventurine threading, a procedure for which the Salviati firm was honored at the 1867 Paris Exhibition. The beaker at right is the most complex technically, with a network of filigree. Known as* vetro a reticello, *this method, originating in the sixteenth century, was lost until the Salviati artisans rediscovered it and reintroduced it in Paris at the 1867 Exhibition. All these techniques became an integral part of the production of the various Salviati enterprises for many years.*

Opposite, above: VETRO A RETICELLO FILIGREE BEAKER (detail)

Opposite, below: BLOWN AVENTURINE BEAKER WITH TURQUOISE GRANZIOLI (detail)

Left to right: The Venice and Murano Glass Company Limited (Salviati & C.)/Salviati Dott. Antonio. VETRO A FILI GOBLET. 1872–95. H. 4⅜". VETRO A FILI CORDIAL. 1872–95. H. 3⅜". VETRO A FILI BEAKER. 1872–95. H. 3⅞". Collection Gardner & Barr, New York

The Venice and Murano Glass Company Limited (Salviati & C.)/
Salviati Dott. Antonio. FLOWER-FORM VASE. 1872–81. H. 7".
The Metropolitan Museum of Art, New York. Gift of
James Jackson Jarves, 1881 (81.8.255) (shown actual size)

Opposite, inset: The Venice and Murano Glass Company Limited
(Salviati & C.)/Salviati Dott. Antonio. VETRO A RETICELLO FINGER BOWL.
1872–95. H. 2", Diam. 4¼". Collection Marjorie Reed Gordon, New York
(shown actual size)

Opposite: VETRO A RETICELLO FINGER BOWL (detail)

The Venice and Murano Glass Company Limited (Salviati & C.)/Salviati Dott. Antonio. COVERED VASE WITH STORKS. 1872–80. H.14½", Diam. 5". The Metropolitan Museum of Art, New York. Gift of James Jackson Jarves, 1881 (81.8.48ab)

Opposite: Salviati Dott. Antonio. Benvenuto Barovier, maker. WINGED DRAGON AND SERPENT VASE. 1877–95. H. 11", Diam. 8". Collection Gardner & Barr, New York *Typical of the exuberant work of Benvenuto Barovier, this technical tour de force easily demonstrates the mastery of nineteenth-century Murano's craftsmen. An identical model is offered in the post-1883 retail catalogue of the Testolini shop.*

Salviati Dott. Antonio/Artisti Barovier. VETRO A RETORTI FINGER BOWL AND UNDER PLATE. 1877–1914. H. 2¾", Diam. 5¼". Collection Marjorie Reed Gordon, New York

Opposite, inset, left to right: The Venice and Murano Glass Company Limited (Salviati & C.)/Salviati Dott. Antonio. VETRO A RETORTI GOBLET. 1872–95. H. 4⅜". VETRO A RETORTI GOBLET. 1872–95. H. 4¾". Collection Marjorie Reed Gordon, New York. VETRO A RETORTI DRAGON STEM GOBLET. 1872–95. H. 8". VETRO A RETORTI GOBLET. 1872–95. H. 4". VETRO A RETORTI LION MASK STEM GOBLET. 1872–95. H. 7". Collection Gardner & Barr, New York. VETRO A RETORTI GOBLET. 1872–95. H. 4⅜". Collection Marjorie Reed Gordon, New York
The molded lion stem was widely used by Venetian and other European glasshouses in the sixteenth and early seventeenth centuries.

Overleaf: Salviati Dott. Antonio/Artisti Barovier. GROUP OF VETRO A RETORTI AND BLOWN AVENTURINE FINGER BOWLS AND UNDER PLATES. 1877–1914. Av. H. 3", Av. Diam. 6". From the collections of Marjorie Reed Gordon and Gardner & Barr, New York

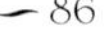

Vetro a retorti Aventurine Dragon Ewer (detail)

Opposite: Artisti Barovier. Giuseppe or Benvenuto Barovier, maker. Vetro a retorti Aventurine Dragon Ewer. 1895–1914. H. 8½", Diam. 7½". Collection Adriana Mnuchin, New York

Right, left to right: Artisti Barovier or Fratelli Toso. Seahorse Ewer. 1895–1914. H. 12". Pegasus and Dolphin Compote. 1895–1914. H. 11". Collection Marjorie Reed Gordon, New York

Below: Pegasus and Dolphin Compote (detail)

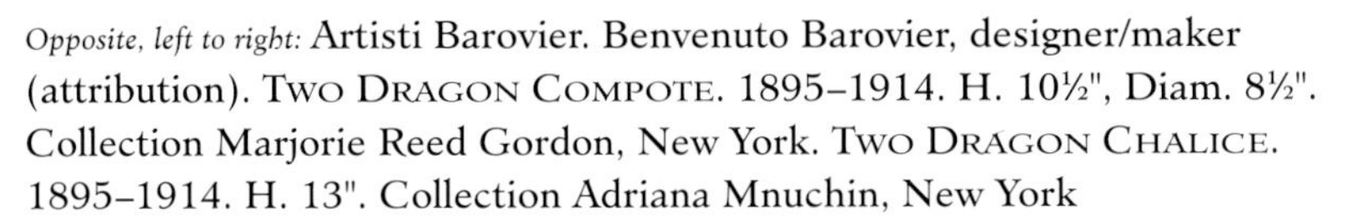

Opposite, left to right: Artisti Barovier. Benvenuto Barovier, designer/maker (attribution). Two Dragon Compote. 1895–1914. H. 10½", Diam. 8½". Collection Marjorie Reed Gordon, New York. Two Dragon Chalice. 1895–1914. H. 13". Collection Adriana Mnuchin, New York

Artisti Barovier or Fratelli Toso. DRAGON COMPOTE. 1895–1914. H. 5¼", Diam. 7½". Collection Marjorie Reed Gordon, New York

Left: DRAGON COMPOTE (detail)

Opposite: Artisti Barovier or Fratelli Toso. FOUR DRAGONS BOWL. 1895–1914. H. 7", Diam. 7½". Collection Marjorie Reed Gordon, New York

Artisti Barovier or Fratelli Toso. DRAGON CANDLESTICKS. 1895–1914. H. 14". Collection Gardner & Barr, New York

Opposite: Artisti Barovier or Fratelli Toso. DRAGON VASES. 1895–1914. H. 16". Collection Marjorie Reed Gordon, New York

PEGASUS COMPOTE (detail)

Opposite, clockwise from the right: Artisti Barovier or Fratelli Toso. PEGASUS COMPOTE WITH VASE. 1895–1914. H. 11¾", Diam. 11⅛". Collection Marjorie Reed Gordon, New York. Artisti Barovier or Fratelli Toso. PEGASUS COMPOTE. 1895–1914. H. 7¼", Diam. 10¼". Collection Gardner & Barr, New York. Artisti Barovier or Fratelli Toso. PEGASUS COMPOTE. 1895–1914. H. 11", Diam. 9¼". Collection Marjorie Reed Gordon, New York

Hippogryph Candlestick (detail)

Opposite, left to right: Artisti Barovier or Fratelli Toso. Dolphin Candlestick. 1895–1914. H. 13". Collection Marjorie Reed Gordon, New York. Three Swans Candlestick. 1895–1914. H. 12½". Hippogryph Candlestick. 1895–1914. H. 12½". Collection Gardner & Barr, New York

The Venice and Murano Glass Company Limited (Salviati & C.)/
Salviati Dott. Antonio. Giuseppe Barovier, designer/maker (attribution).
CORINTHIAN SPANGLED VASE. 1872–80. H. 6⅛", Diam. 4⅜".
The Metropolitan Museum of Art, New York. Gift of James Jackson
Jarves, 1881 (81.8.74) (shown actual size)
The form of this vase was inspired by late seventeenth-, early eighteenth-century Venetian glass copies of ancient Greek pottery kantharos vases.

The Venice and Murano Glass Company Limited (Salviati & C.)/Salviati Dott. Antonio. Giuseppe Barovier, designer/maker (attribution). CORINTHIAN SPANGLED VASE. 1872–80. H. 11¾", Diam. 5".
The Metropolitan Museum of Art, New York. Gift of James Jackson Jarves, 1881 (81.8.125)

Artisti Barovier or Fratelli Toso. FLOWER VASE WITH THREE SPOUTS. 1895–1914. H. 8¼". Collection Gardner & Barr, New York
Inspired by sixteenth and seventeenth century Venetian and Spanish prototypes, elaborate vessels like this were produced in many colors and sizes, often with a number of spouts and handles.

Opposite: Salviati Dott. Antonio/Artisti Barovier or Fratelli Toso. OPALESCENT VASE WITH APPLIED MASKS. 1877–1914. H. 10⅛". Collection Gardner & Barr, New York

Artisti Barovier or Fratelli Toso. CANDLESTICKS. 1895–1914. H. 11½".
Collection Marjorie Reed Gordon, New York

Opposite, left to right: Salviati Dott. Antonio/Artisti Barovier or Fratelli Toso. CORNUCOPIA VASE. 1877–1914. H. 12". Collection Gardner & Barr, New York. VASE WITH APPLIED MASKS. 1877–1914. H. 10". Collection Adriana Mnuchin, New York. SHELL FORM VASE. 1877–1914. H. 10½". Collection Gardner & Barr, New York

This line drawing is taken from the post-1883 Testolini shop's retail sales catalogue.

Right: Fratelli Toso (attribution). MOSAIC GLASS VASE WITH DRAGON/BIRD FOOT. 1877–1914. H. 8", Diam. 3¾". Collection Alessandro Zoppi, Antichita Cesana, Venice
The use of free-floating murrhine suggests Fratelli Toso as the manufacturer of this vase. (Shown actual size)

Opposite: Salviati Dott. Antonio/Artisti Barovier or Fratelli Toso. SCALLOP SHELL VASE WITH SEA-HORSE HANDLES. 1877–1914. H. 12½". Collection Alessandro Zoppi, Antichita Cesana, Venice

Salviati Dott. Antonio/Artisti Barovier or Fratelli Toso. DOLPHIN COMPOTE. 1877–1914. H. 6", Diam. 8¾".
Collection Alessandro Zoppi, Antichita Cesana, Venice

Opposite, left to right: Salviati Dott. Antonio/Artisti Barovier or Fratelli Toso. TWO DRAGON VASE. 1877–1914. H. 10".
DRAGON VASE. 1877–1914. H. 7½". Collection Alessandro Zoppi, Antichita Cesana, Venice

Previous pages: Salviati Dott. Antonio/Artisti Barovier or Fratelli Toso. GROUP OF TWENTY-ONE GOBLETS. 1877–1914. Av. H. 6", Av. Diam. 2". From the collections of Marjorie Reed Gordon and Gardner & Barr, New York
Goblets were a huge commercial success for the Venetian glass shops. They were expensive and sold in large sets to visiting tourists and exported throughout the world. The goblet designs ranged from simple sixteenth century-style forms to elaborate nineteenth-century tours de force.

Above and below: Goblet stem details

Opposite: Salviati Dott. Antonio/Artisti Barovier. SIXTEENTH CENTURY-STYLE VASE. 1877–95. H. 6½". Collection Gardner & Barr, New York

Artisti Barovier. SPIRAL STEM COMPOTE. 1885–1914. H. 9". Collection Usha Subramaniam, New York

Opposite, left to right: Salviati Dott. Antonio/Artist Barovier. FLOWER FORM VASE. 1877–1914. H. 10¼". VASE WITH BLUE RING HANDLES. 1877–1914. H. 9¼". VASE WITH ELABORATE CHAIN STEM. 1877–1914. H. 8½". VASE WITH APPLIED THREADING. 1877–1914. H. 11". VASE WITH INDENTATIONS. 1877–1914. H. 8¾". Collection Gardner & Barr, New York
The Barovier family began producing extremely light, pale straw-colored sixteenth century-style glass for the Salviati shops in the 1870s. It was not until 1895 and beyond that this production gained widespread popularity.

Fratelli Toso. MOSAIC GLASS PITCHER. 1900–1914. H. 4⅞".
Collection Gardner & Barr, New York
By copying the sixteenth-century millefiori technique, revived at Salviati's glassworks, the Fratelli Toso, Murano's oldest glasshouse, produced a large and commercially successful series of beautifully crafted mosaic glass objects in the years prior to World War I.

Opposite: Fratelli Toso. MONUMENTAL MOSAIC GLASS VASE. 1900–1914. H. 14".
Collection Gardner & Barr, New York

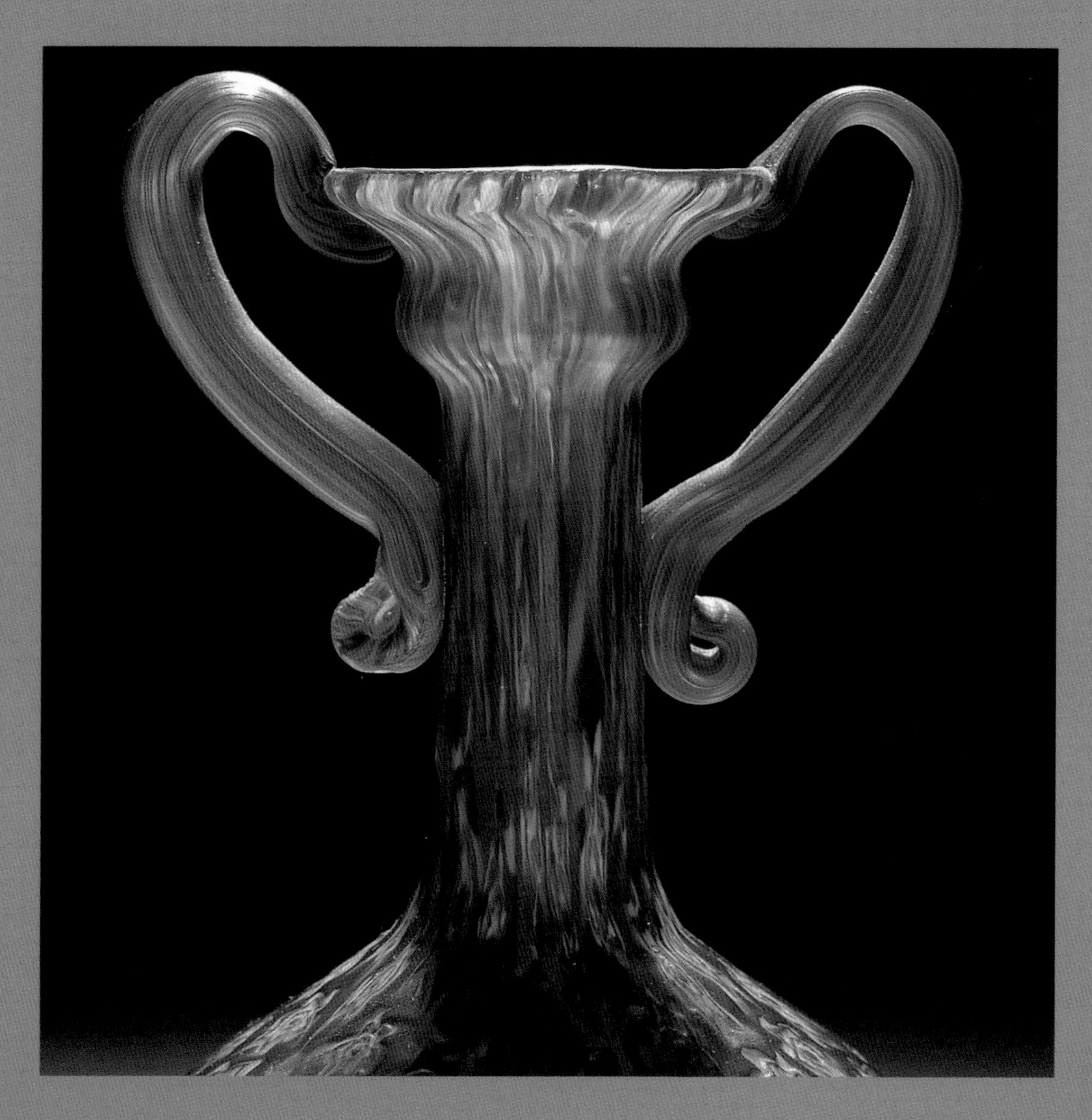

Previous pages: Fratelli Toso. Group of Nine Mosaic Glass Vases and Pitchers. 1900–1914. H. from 2" to 6". Collection Gardner & Barr, New York
Sometimes using murrhine produced from a single cane, but more often from two canes of contrasting, but complementary colors, the Fratelli Toso produced a vast range of mosaic glass objects, such as vases, pitchers, teapots, chandeliers, and lamps in the early years of the twentieth century.

Above and opposite: Mosaic glass details

Artisti Barovier. MOSAIC GLASS HANGING LAMP. 1900–1914.
H. 6¾". Collection Gardner & Barr, New York

Opposite: MOSAIC GLASS HANGING LAMP (detail)

Notes

1. The traditional glass furnaces of Murano burned wood until the mid-twentieth century. The beech wood that grew on the western shores of the Adriatic in Dalmatia and Istria burned at a high temperature and was therefore the fuel of choice for the Murano glassblowers. It was transported across the Adriatic on specially built barges called *trabaccoli.*

2. *fu Bartolomeo* in Venetian vernacular indicates that Antonio Salviati is the son of Bartolomeo Salviati, deceased.

3. A *stabilimento* was a retail showroom, often of vast proportions, sometimes occupying an entire palazzo.

4. The conscious re-creation of objects from an idealized past.

5. Sarpellon, Giovanni et al., *Salviati: Il suo vetro e i suoi uomini, 1858–1987* (Venice: La Stamperia di Venezia, 1989), p. 13.

6. Noted and named for its remarkable crystal staircase, the *Escalier de Crystal* was a shop in Paris's Palais-Royal area that specialized in glassware. Founded in 1802 by a Mme Desarnaud, by 1818 the shop had become the glassware supplier to Charles X, king of France. Changing hands several times during the course of the nineteenth century, in 1854 it was owned and managed by the partners LaHoche and Pannier. The shop did not manufacture its merchandise but rather was supplied by forty to fifty outside craftsmen. In the 1860s it was the exclusive representative of Venetian glass in France.

7. In the fifteenth century, Murano was the luxurious playground of Venetian aristocracy. When, two hundred years later, the patricians deserted Murano for new villas on the mainland, many of Murano's abandoned palaces were converted to glass factories and many eventually burned. By the mid-nineteenth century the sole survivor of Murano's halcyon days was the once magnificent palazzo Da Mula, by then a functioning glass factory. It was the perfect spot for Antonio Salviati to set up the large furnaces he needed to realize his dream of resurrecting Murano's languishing glass industry. The Compagnia di Venezia e Murano took over when Salviati was bought out by his British partners in 1877. In 1910 they ceded the palazzo to Andrea Rioda, who, from 1911 until 1921, kept the glassworks producing under his own name, Andrea Rioda & C. After Rioda's death in 1921 the palazzo became the glassworks of the new Cappellin Venini & C. which was dissolved in 1925. That year Paolo Venini became the sole owner of the venerable old palazzo and formed the Soffiati Muranesi Venini & C.

8. John Ruskin, *The Stones of Venice,* vol. 2 (London, 1853), pp. 168–69.

9. Alternatively a cylindrical glass bubble attached to a blowpipe was rolled over the fused filigrana canes and they were picked up in this manner.

10. Sarpellon, p. 14.

11. Venetian terminology can be confusing. In this case the term "graffito" was abandoned and currently "fenicio" is used to describe this technique of combed festoons. We will continue this usage and refer to the imitation ancient Phoenician glass later produced by the Compagnia di Venezia e Murano and the Fratelli Toso as Phoenician-style.

12. Abbot Zanetti's latest project, a bimonthly journal devoted to the Murano glass industry, inaugurated in 1867.

13. "Modern Venetian Glass," *The Art Journal* (London,1866), p. 290.

14. Paul Hollister,"The Remarkable Glass Gift of James Jackson Jarves, A Collector in a Hurry," *The Acorn* (n.p.,n.d.).

15. Rosa Barovier Mentasti, *Il vetro veneziano* (Milan: Electa Spa Milano, 1982), p. 207, caption for 206. Other virtually identical chalices are in the collection of The Corning Museum of Glass, Corning, New York, and the Murano Glass Museum, Murano.

16. The technique of forming a two-layered mass and blowing it into a desired shape was used to produce "filigrana" as well "millifiori" glass from the sixteenth century on. See "filigrana" glass window.

17. Giovanni Sarpellon, *Miniature Masterpieces: Mosaic Glass 1838–1924* (Munich: Prestel Munich-New York: 1995), p. 101.

18. James Jackson Jarves, "Ancient and Modern Glass of Murano," *Harper's New York Monthly Magazine 64* (Dec.1881–May 1882), p. 189.

19. *La Voce di Murano* (Dec.15, 1878) from Sarpellon, *Miniature Masterpieces* (Munich: Prestel Munich-New York, 1995), p. 102.

20. Most large Venetian glass companies had, in addition to their huge shops on the Grand Canal, smaller showrooms on the Piazza San Marco, ostensibly to attract the tourist trade to the larger stores.

21. Core forming is a process involving the manipulation of hot, softened glass around a core of clay and organic matter which, after the glass has cooled, is removed.

22. Called in Murano German red due to its invention there, or American red, thanks to the new color's partisans.

23. The participating businesses were Salviati & C., Jesurum & C., the Venice Art Co., and Pagliarin & Franco.

24. AMF 1914, the logo and date of the Fiera mostra dei fiori.

List of Plates

PER. 1866–72. H. 15¾". VETRO A FILI AVENTURINE DECANTER WITH STOPPER. 1866–72. H. 11". DECANTER WITH BLUE RIGAREE. 1866–72. H. 9". STRAW-COLORED DECANTER. 1866–72. H. 9". DECANTER WITH APPLIED PRUNTS AND STOPPER. 1866–72. H. 10". Collection Marjorie Reed Gordon, New York

Page 54 Left to right: Societa Anonima per azioni Salviati & C. VETRO A FILI DECANTER. 1866–72. H. 10¾". Collection Marjorie Reed Gordon, New York. PHOENICIAN-STYLE DECANTER. 1866–72. H. 12". Collection Gardner & Barr, New York

Page 55 Societa Anonima per azioni Salviati & C. COVERED BOWL. 1866–72. H. 4¾". Collection Robert Conant, New York

Page 56 Societa Anonima per azioni Salviati & C. VASE. 1866–68. H. 9⅞". Victoria and Albert Museum, London. Purchased from Salviati in 1868 (905–1868)

Page 57 Societa Anonima per azioni Salviati & C. SERPENT STEM GOBLET. 1866. H. 7¼". Victoria and Albert Museum, London. Gift of Salviati & C., 1937 (C39–1937)

Page 58 Left to right: Societa Anonima per azioni Salviati & C. ENAMELED GOBLET. 1866–72. H. 4⅛", Diam. 3⅝". ENAMELED GOBLET. 1866–72. H. 4¼", Diam. 4¼". Collection Gardner & Barr, New York. ENAMELED CUP AND SAUCER. 1866–72. H. 3", Diam. 5⅝". Collection Marjorie Reed Gordon, New York

Page 59 Societa Anonima per azioni Salviati & C. PHOENICIAN-STYLE TAZZA. 1866–69. H. 6". Victoria and Albert Museum, London. Purchased from Salviati (67–1870)

Page 60 Societa Anonima per azioni Salviati & C. ENAMELED GOBLET. 1866–72. H. 7⅜", Diam. 4¾". The Metropolitan Museum of Art, New York. Gift of James Jackson Jarves, 1881 (81.8.220)

Page 61 Societa Anonima per azioni Salviati & C. Leopoldo Bearzotti, decorator (attribution). ENAMELED CHALICE. 1866–72. H. 13⅝". Collection Gardner & Barr, New York

Page 62 Salviati Dott. Antonio/Artisti Barovier. Giuseppe or Benvenuto Barovier, maker. BLOWN AVENTURINE VASE. 1877–1914. H. 9⅞". Collection Gardner & Barr, New York

Page 63 The Venice and Murano Glass Company Limited (Salviati & C.)/ Salviati Dott. Antonio. SCALLOP SHELL EWER. 1872–95. H. 8⅛", Diam. 3⅞". Collection Gardner & Barr, New York

Page 65 The Venice and Murano Glass Company Limited. Vincenzo Moretti, maker. MURRHINE GLASS VASE. 1878. H. 5½", Diam. 5". Mark: murrhine bearing initial "V" superimposed over initial "M". Collection Gardner & Barr, New York

Page 67 Left to right: Fratelli Toso. MOSAIC GLASS PITCHER. 1900–1914. H. 5¾". The Venice and Murano Glass Company Limited (Salviati & C.)/ Salviati Dott. Antonio. Giuseppe or Benvenuto Barovier, maker. MOSAIC GLASS PITCHER. 1872–95. H. 5½". Collection Gardner & Barr, New York

Page 68 The Venice and Murano Glass Company Limited (Salviati & C.). Giuseppe or Benvenuto Barovier, maker. MOSAIC GLASS VASE. 1872. H. 5". Victoria and Albert Museum, London. Purchased from maker, 1873

Page 69 The Venice and Murano Glass Company Limited (Salviati & C.)/ Salviati Dott. Antonio. Giuseppe or Benvenuto Barovier, maker. MOSAIC GLASS VASE WITH COVER. 1872–81. H. 12", Diam. 7". The Metropolitan Museum of Art, New York. Gift of James Jackson Jarves, 1881 (81.8.213ab)

Page 70 The Venice and Murano Glass Company Limited. EWER. 1881–1910. H. 6⅛". Collection Gardner & Barr, New York

Page 71 Left to right: The Venice and Murano Glass Company Limited. Vincenzo Moretti, designer/maker. PHOENICIAN-STYLE PITCHER. 1881–1910. H. 3⅞". PHOENICIAN-STYLE VASE. 1881–1910. H. 9". PHOENICIAN-STYLE VASE. 1881–1910. H. 5⅝". PHOENICIAN-STYLE PITCHER. 1881–1910. H. 6¼". Collection Gardner & Barr, New York

Page 72 Left to right: The Venice and Murano Glass Company Limited (Salviati & C.)/Salviati Dott. Antonio. VETRO A RETORTI PITCHER. 1872–95. H. 13". VETRO A RETORTI PITCHER. 1872–95. H. 7¼". Collection Gardner & Barr, New York. VETRO A FILI AVENTURINE PITCHER. 1872–95. H. 13½". Collection Adriana Mnuchin, New York

Page 73 Salviati Dott. Antonio/Artisti Barovier. VETRO A FILI AVENTURINE FOOTED COMPOTE. 1877–1914. H. 7¼", Diam. 10⅝". Collection Gardner & Barr, New York

Page 74 Left to right: The Venice and Murano Glass Company Limited (Salviati & C.)/Salviati Dott. Antonio. PUMPKIN-SHAPED BOWL. 1872–95. H. 4⅛", Diam. 7". OCTAGONAL BOWL. 1872–95. H. 2⅞", Diam. 4⅛". Collection Gardner & Barr, New York

Page 75 Left to right: The Venice and Murano Glass Company Limited (Salviati & C.). Yellow Vase. 1872–77. H. 7¼". Yellow Screziato (multicolor) Vase. 1872–77. H. 5¾". Screziato (multicolor) Vase. 1872–77. H. 5¾". Marbleized Vase. 1872–77. H. 5½". Collection Gardner & Barr, New York

Page 76 Left to right: Societa Anonima per azioni Salviati & C./The Venice and Murano Glass Company Limited (Salviati & C.)/Salviati Dott. Antonio or Artisti Barovier. Phoenician-style Beaker. 1869–95. H. 3¼". Vetro a retorti Beaker. 1867–95. H. 3⅛". Blown Aventurine Beaker with Turquoise Granzioli. 1871–1914. H. 3¾". Vetro a fili Beaker with Applied Aventurine Threading and Prunts. 1867–1914. H. 3¼". Vetro a reticello Beaker. 1867–1914. H. 3⅝". Collection Gardner & Barr, New York

Page 77 Left to right: The Venice and Murano Glass Company Limited (Salviati & C.)/Salviati Dott. Antonio. Vetro a fili Goblet. 1872–95. H. 4⅜". Vetro a fili Cordial. 1872–95. H. 3⅜". Vetro a fili Beaker. 1872–95. H. 3⅞". Collection Gardner & Barr, New York

Page 78 The Venice and Murano Glass Company Limited (Salviati & C.)/ Salviati Dott. Antonio. Vetro a reticello Finger bowl. 1872–95. H. 2", Diam. 4¼". Collection Marjorie Reed Gordon, New York

Page 79 The Venice and Murano Glass Company Limited (Salviati & C.)/ Salviati Dott. Antonio. Flower-form Vase. 1872–81. H. 7". The Metropolitan Museum of Art, New York. Gift of James Jackson Jarves. 1881 (81.8.255)

Page 80 The Venice and Murano Glass Company Limited (Salviati & C.)/ Salviati Dott. Antonio. Covered Vase with Storks. 1872–80. H.14½", Diam. 5". The Metropolitan Museum of Art, New York. Gift of James Jackson Jarves, 1881 (81.8.48ab)

Page 81 Salviati Dott. Antonio. Benvenuto Barovier, maker. Winged Dragon and Serpent Vase. 1877–95. H. 11", Diam. 8". Collection Gardner & Barr, New York

Page 82 Left to right: The Venice and Murano Glass Company Limited (Salviati & C.)/Salviati Dott. Antonio. Vetro a retorti Goblet. 1872–95. H. 4⅜". Vetro a retorti Goblet. 1872–95. H. 4¾". Collection Marjorie Reed Gordon, New York. Vetro a retorti Dragon Stem Goblet. 1872–95. H. 8". Vetro a retorti Goblet. 1872–95. H. 4". Vetro a retorti Lion Mask Stem Goblet. 1872–95. H. 7". Collection Gardner & Barr, New York. Vetro a retorti Goblet. 1872–95. H. 4⅜". Collection Marjorie Reed Gordon, New York

Page 83 Salviati Dott. Antonio/Artisti Barovier. Vetro a retorti Finger bowl and Under plate. 1877–1914. H. 2¾", Diam. 5¼". Collection Marjorie Reed Gordon, New York

Pages 84–85 Salviati Dott. Antonio/ Artisti Barovier. Group of Vetro a retorti and Blown Aventurine Finger bowls and Under plates. 1877–1914. Av. H. 3", Av. Diam. 6". From the collections of Marjorie Reed Gordon and Gardner & Barr, New York

Page 87 Artisti Barovier. Giuseppe or Benvenuto Barovier, maker. Vetro a retorti Aventurine Dragon Ewer. 1895–1914. H. 8½", Diam. 7½". Collection Adriana Mnuchin, New York

Page 88 Left to right: Artisti Barovier. Benvenuto Barovier, designer/maker (attribution). Two Dragon Compote. 1895–1914. H. 10½", Diam. 8½". Collection Marjorie Reed Gordon, New York. Two Dragon Chalice. 1895–1914. H. 13". Collection Adriana Mnuchin, New York

Page 89 Left to right: Artisti Barovier or Fratelli Toso. Seahorse Ewer. 1895–1914. H. 12". Pegasus and Dolphin Compote. 1895–1914. H. 11". Collection Marjorie Reed Gordon, New York

Page 90 Artisti Barovier or Fratelli Toso. Four Dragons Bowl. 1895–1914. H. 7", Diam. 7½". Collection Marjorie Reed Gordon, New York

Page 91 Artisti Barovier or Fratelli Toso. Dragon Compote. 1895–1914. H. 5¼", Diam. 7½". Collection Marjorie Reed Gordon, New York

Page 92 Artisti Barovier or Fratelli Toso. Dragon Candlesticks. 1895–1914. H. 14". Collection Gardner & Barr, New York

Page 93 Artisti Barovier or Fratelli Toso. Dragon Vases. 1895–1914. H. 16". Collection Marjorie Reed Gordon, New York

Page 95 Clockwise from the right: Artisti Barovier or Fratelli Toso. Pegasus Compote with Vase. 1895–1914. H. 11¾", Diam. 11⅛". Collection Marjorie Reed Gordon, New York. Artisti Barovier or Fratelli Toso. Pegasus Compote. 1895–1914. H. 7¼", Diam. 10¼". Collection Gardner &

Barr, New York. Artisti Barovier or Fratelli Toso. PEGASUS COMPOTE. 1895–1914. H. 11", Diam. 9¼". Collection Marjorie Reed Gordon, New York

Page 96 Left to right: Artisti Barovier or Fratelli Toso. DOLPHIN CANDLESTICK. 1895–1914. H. 13". Collection Marjorie Reed Gordon, New York. THREE SWANS CANDLESTICK. 1895–1914. H. 12½". HIPPOGRYPH CANDLESTICK. 1895–1914. H. 12½". Collection Gardner & Barr, New York

Page 98 The Venice and Murano Glass Company Limited (Salviati & C.)/ Salviati Dott. Antonio. Giuseppe Barovier, designer/maker (attribution). CORINTHIAN SPANGLED VASE. 1872–80. H. 6⅛", Diam. 4⅜". The Metropolitan Museum of Art, New York. Gift of James Jackson Jarves, 1881 (81.8.74)

Page 99 The Venice and Murano Glass Company Limited (Salviati & C.)/ Salviati Dott. Antonio. Giuseppe Barovier, designer/maker (attribution). CORINTHIAN SPANGLED VASE. 1872–80. H. 11¾", Diam. 5". The Metropolitan Museum of Art, New York. Gift of James Jackson Jarves, 1881 (81.8.125)

Page 100 Artisti Barovier or Fratelli Toso. FLOWER VASE WITH THREE SPOUTS. 1895–1914. H. 8¼". Collection Gardner & Barr, New York

Page 101 Salviati Dott. Antonio/Artisti Barovier or Fratelli Toso. OPALESCENT VASE WITH APPLIED MASKS. 1877–1914. H. 10⅛". Collection Gardner & Barr, New York

Page 102 Left to right: Salviati Dott. Antonio/Artisti Barovier or Fratelli Toso. CORNUCOPIA VASE. 1877–1914. H. 12". Collection Gardner & Barr, New York. VASE WITH APPLIED MASKS. 1877–1914. H. 10". Collection Adriana Mnuchin, New York. SHELL FORM VASE. 1877–1914. H. 10½". Collection Gardner & Barr, New York

Page 103 Artisti Barovier or Fratelli Toso. CANDLESTICKS. 1895–1914. H. 11½". Collection Marjorie Reed Gordon, New York

Page 104 Fratelli Toso (attribution). MOSAIC GLASS VASE WITH DRAGON/ BIRD FOOT. 1877–1914. H. 8", Diam. 3¾". Collection Alessandro Zoppi, Antichita Cesana, Venice

Page 105 Salviati Dott. Antonio/Artisti Barovier or Fratelli Toso. SCALLOP SHELL VASE WITH SEAHORSE HANDLES. 1877–1914. H. 12½". Collection Alessandro Zoppi, Antichita Cesana, Venice

Page 106 Salviati Dott. Antonio/Artisti Barovier or Fratelli Toso. DOLPHIN COMPOTE. 1877–1914. H. 6", Diam. 8¾". Collection Alessandro Zoppi, Antichita Cesana, Venice

Page 107 Left to right: Salviati Dott. Antonio/Artisti Barovier or Fratelli Toso. TWO DRAGON VASE. 1877–1914. H. 10". DRAGON VASE. 1877–1914. H. 7½". Collection Alessandro Zoppi, Antichita Cesana, Venice

Pages 108–109 Salviati Dott. Antonio/ Artisti Barovier or Fratelli Toso. GROUP OF TWENTY-ONE GOBLETS. 1877–1914. Av. H. 6", Av. Diam. 2". From the collections of Marjorie Reed Gordon and Gardner & Barr, New York

Page 111 Salviati Dott. Antonio/Artisti Barovier. SIXTEENTH CENTURY-STYLE VASE. 1877–95. H. 6½". Collection Gardner & Barr, New York

Page 112 Left to right: Salviati Dott. Antonio/Artist Barovier. FLOWER FORM VASE. 1877–1914. H. 10¼". VASE WITH BLUE RING HANDLES. 1877–1914. H. 9¼". VASE WITH ELABORATE CHAIN STEM. 1877–1914. H. 8½". VASE WITH APPLIED THREADING. 1877–1914. H. 11". VASE WITH INDENTATIONS. 1877–1914. H. 8¾". Collection Gardner & Barr, New York

Page 113 Artisti Barovier. SPIRAL STEM COMPOTE. 1885–1914. H. 9". Collection Usha Subramaniam, New York

Page 114 Fratelli Toso. MONUMENTAL MOSAIC GLASS VASE. 1900–1914. H. 14". Collection Gardner & Barr, New York

Page 115 Fratelli Toso. MOSAIC GLASS PITCHER. 1900–1914. H. 4⅞". Collection Gardner & Barr, New York

Pages 116-117 Fratelli Toso. GROUP OF NINE MOSAIC GLASS VASES AND PITCHERS. 1900–1914. H. from 2" to 6". Collection Gardner & Barr, New York

Page 121 Artisti Barovier. MOSAIC GLASS HANGING LAMP. 1900–1914. H. 6¾". Collection Gardner & Barr, New York

Page 128 Societa Anonima per azioni Salviati & C. PHOENICIAN-STYLE VASE. 1866–72. H. 6¾". Collection Gardner & Barr, New York

Acknowledgments

Societa Anonima per azioni Salviati & C. PHOENICIAN-STYLE VASE. 1866–72. H. 6¾". Collection Gardner & Barr, New York

I wish to thank Robert Conant, Adriana Mnuchin, Usha Subramaniam, and Alessandro Zoppi for the privilege of photographing their superb collections. Attilia Dorigato, Curator, The Murano Glass Museum, Murano; Reino Liefkes, Deputy Curator of Ceramics and Glass, The Victoria & Albert Museum, London; and Jessie McNab, Associate Curator, The Metropolitan Museum of Art, New York, all deserve recognition for their help in giving easy access to their museum's collections and for their generosity in sharing their wealth of knowledge. And to James Van Wert, Jeanette Hayhurst, Kenneth Paul Lesko, Giorgio Raccanello, and Richard Weissenberger my thanks for the use of their invaluable documentation, and Berenika A. Cipkus for her incisive translations of the Italian texts.

SHELDON BARR

I wish to express heartfelt thanks to my mother, Anne Kahn, whose passion for beautiful things was passed on to me at an early age. To my husband, Ellery, whose support, patience, and encouragement have enhanced both my collection and my life, thank you, my love.

MARJORIE REED GORDON